THEMATIC UNIT
CHRISTMAS

Written by Iretta Sitts Graube

Illustrated by Cheryl Buhler and Keith Vasconcelles

Teacher Created Materials, Inc.
P.O. Box 1040
Huntington Beach, CA 92647
©1992 Teacher Created Materials, Inc.
Made in U.S.A.

ISBN 1-55734-259-8

Table of Contents

Introduction

Christmas contains a captivating whole language, thematic unit. Its 80 exciting pages are filled with a wide variety of lesson ideas and activities designed for use with primary children. At its core are three high-quality children's literature selections, *Night Tree*, *The Wild Christmas Reindeer*, and *The Polar Express*. For each of these books, activities are included which set the stage for reading, encourage the enjoyment of the book, and extend the concepts gained. In addition, the theme is connected to the curriculum with activities in language arts, math, science, social studies, geography, art, music, movement, and life skills. Many of these activities encourage cooperative learning. Suggestions and patterns for games and ideas for the bulletin boards are additional time savers for the busy teacher. Furthermore, directions for making a class pillow, wall hanging, or quilt allow the students to produce products that can be shared beyond the classroom. All of these activities combine to make this book a very complete teacher resource.

This thematic unit includes:

❑ **literature selections**—summaries of three children's books with related lessons (complete with reproducible pages) that cross the curriculum

❑ **poetry**—suggested selections and lessons enabling students to write and publish their own works

❑ **planning guides**—suggestions for sequencing lessons each day of the unit

❑ **language experience ideas**—daily suggestions as well as activities across the curriculum, including Big Books

❑ **bulletin board ideas**—suggestions and plans for student-created and/or interactive bulletin boards

❑ **homework suggestions**—extending the unit to the child's home

❑ **curriculum connections**—in language arts, math, science, social studies, geography, art, music, movement, and life skills

❑ **group projects**—to foster cooperative learning

❑ **a culminating activity**—which requires students to synthesize their learning to produce a product or engage in an activity that can be shared with others

❑ **a bibliography**—suggesting additional literature and nonfiction books on the theme

---

To keep this valuable resource intact so that it can be used year after year, you may wish to punch holes in the pages and store them in a three-ring binder.

Introduction *(cont.)*

Why Whole Language?

A whole language approach involves children in using all modes of communication: reading, writing, listening, observing, illustrating, experiencing, and doing. Communication skills are interconnected and integrated into lessons that emphasize the whole of language rather than isolating its parts. The lessons revolve around selected literature. Reading is not taught as a separate subject from writing and spelling, for example. A child reads, writes (spelling appropriately for his/her level), speaks, listens, etc. in response to a literature experience introduced by the teacher. In this way, language skills grow naturally, stimulated by involvement and interest in the topic at hand.

Why Thematic Planning?

One very useful tool for implementing an integrated whole language program is thematic planning. By choosing a theme with correlating literature selections for a unit of study, a teacher can plan activities throughout the day that lead to a cohesive, in-depth study of the topic. Students will be practicing and applying their skills in meaningful context. Consequently, they will tend to learn and retain more. Both teachers and students will be freed from a day that is broken into unrelated segments of isolated drill and practice.

Why Cooperative Learning?

Besides academic skills and content, students need to learn social skills. No longer can this area of development be taken for granted. Students must learn to work cooperatively in groups in order to function well in modern society. Group activities should be a regular part of school life, and teachers should consciously include social objectives as well as academic objectives in the planning. For example, a group working together to write a report may need to select a leader. The teacher should make the objectives clear to the students and monitor the qualities of good leader-follower group interaction just as he/she would state and monitor the academic goals of the project.

Why Big Books?

An excellent, cooperative, whole language activity is the production of Big Books. Groups of students or the whole class can apply their language skills, content knowledge, and creativity to produce a Big Book that can become a part of the classroom to be read and reread. These books make excellent culminating projects for sharing beyond the classroom with parents, librarians, and other classes. Big Books can be produced in many ways. This thematic unit book includes directions for one method you may choose.

Why Journals?

Each day your students should have the opportunity to write in a journal. They may respond to a book, write about a personal experience, or answer a general "question of the day" posed by the teacher. Students should be encouraged to refer to the posted vocabulary list to check their spelling. The cumulative journal provides an excellent means of documenting writing progress.

Night Tree
by Eve Bunting
Summary

This family has a unique Christmas tradition. Deep in a moonlit forest they have a special tree. They return to this tree every year to decorate it for all the forest creatures and to rekindle the Christmas spirit in their own way. The beautiful watercolor illustrations and the touching story make this a book children love to hear.

The outline below is a suggested plan for using the various activities presented in this unit. You may adapt the ideas to meet specific needs in your classroom.

Sample Plan

Day 1

- Post pictures of different types of trees on bulletin board. Discuss.
- Share the history of Christmas trees. (page 15)
- Read *Night Tree*, stopping at the page where they find their tree. What will the family do next? Discuss.
- Finish reading the book. Discuss.
- Begin making a Big Book. (page 8)

Day 2

- Continue work on the Big Book with story sequence strips. (page 8)
- Read the Big Book to partners.
- List "Animal Habitats." (page 58)
- Make Stand Up Christmas Trees. (page 15)
- Write about your tree. (page 15)
- Do Christmas tree math. (page 53)
- Learn song "Let's All Decorate the Night Tree." (page 70)

Day 3

- Introduce Tagging Christmas Trees. (page 10)
- Find out where Christmas trees come from. (page 11)
- Do Geography questionnaire. (page 12)
- Play Wildlife Concentration. (page 58)
- Make Pop-Up Place Cards. (page 62)
- Continue singing "Let's All Decorate the Night Tree."
- Make Fox Sandwiches. (page 72)

Day 4

- Complete What Do Animals Eat Chart? (page 44)
- Write sentence strips from the chart. (page 44)
- Play Wildlife Bingo. (page 59)
- Color the Tree. (page 9)

Day 5

- Do Ornament Placement. (page 45)
- Make a stained glass Christmas tree. (page 63)
- Enjoy storytelling with your stained glass tree. (page 63)
- Make Christmas paper crackers. (page 64)
- Decorate Popcorn Christmas Trees. (page 16)

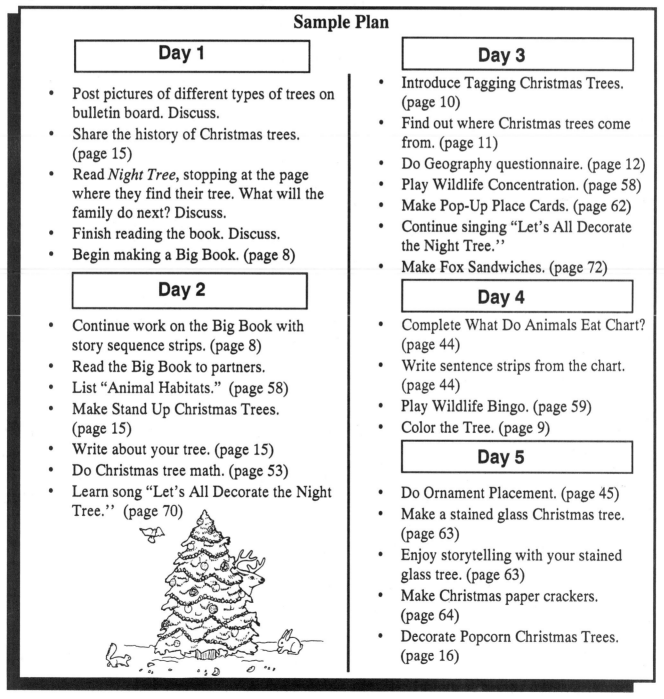

Overview of Activities

Setting the Stage

1. Find pictures of coniferous and deciduous trees and post them on the bulletin board. Check out books on trees and pinecones. Have them available for students to read.

2. Discuss the history of Christmas trees. (page 15)

3. Take a walk around the school grounds or to a local park and try to identify the trees. Discuss what was seen.

4. Contact a local Christmas tree farm and arrange a visit. If you don't live in an area that grows Christmas trees, find out where Christmas trees come from that are shipped to your area. (page 11)

5. Have a science center with small branches of various evergreen trees. Supply a magnifying glass and look at the differences in the needles. Have children identify the different types of evergreen trees after examining their branches. Have a tree identification book handy to help them label the branches. Supply 3" X 5" note cards for use in labeling the trees. Collect pine cones to place in the science center.

6. Send home the letter to parents about stocking stuffers. (page 78)

Enjoying the Book

1. Read part of the book. Stop reading when you get to the page where the family finds the tree. Ask the children what they think the family will do next. Discuss.

2. Finish reading the book. Discuss this family and their tradition. Ask children how it differs from what their families do.

3. Discuss the order of events in the story. Make Big Books with the story sequence strips on page 8. Have the students read the Big Books to each other or place pages on a bulletin board or in a hallway in the correct order.

4. Look at the illustrations in the book from the illustrators perspective. Was the illustrator up high looking down or down low looking up? Identify each page from a perspective viewpoint.

5. Make a picture pretending you are up on the ceiling looking down at the classroom. How would it look? Let the children stand on chairs and tables and look down at an object on the floor to get a feeling of drawing something as they look down at it.

6. Find out where children may have seen animals from the story. Use the chart on page 58 to determine animal habitats.

Overview of Activities *(cont.)*

Extending the Book

1. List all the animals found on the last page of the book. On a chart, group the animals by color, number of legs, method of moving, etc.

2. Ask the children: If you put out food tonight at your house, which of the animals living in your area would possibly come eat it?

3. Make a pine cone bird feeder. Tie a string around the cone to enable you to hang it in a tree. Roll a pine cone in thin sugary icing. Sprinkle sesame seeds or sunflower seeds on the pine cone. Hang the cone from a tree. Record which birds come to eat and what time of day they come.

Animal	Day-Time
mouse	12/5—night

4. Find a tree on the school grounds. Decorate it with strings of popcorn, cranberries, and apples. Scatter nuts and bread crumbs under the tree. Check everyday to see what is missing. Look for footprints to help you discover which animals might have visited the tree. Keep a record of your findings.

5. Let the children decorate their own popcorn Christmas tree and feed themselves! (page 16) Write down the directions for making the popcorn tree. Let each take the directions home and teach their families how to make their own popcorn trees.

Making a Big Book with Story Sequence Strips

Materials: An enlarged copy of the sentences at the bottom of this page for every four children; 9" X 12" construction paper in white or various light colors; scissors; stapler or book binder; a variety of materials for children to use to illustrate the book, i.e. crayons, watercolors, oil crayons, colored chalk

Directions: Reread the book. Discuss the sequence of events in the story. Arrange the children in groups of four. Each group will make one book. Read the sentence strips together. Cut apart the sentence strips and glue each strip to a sheet of construction paper. Divide up the pages so each child will illustrate 2 to 3 pages. Put the pages in order so that it tells the story. Read the story again to make sure you have the pages in the correct order. Make a cover for the book. Include a title page at the beginning telling the book's author and students' names as illustrators. Number the pages by placing the correct number in the lower center of each page. Staple or bind the book together. Have students read it to other classmates and show the illustrations. Place the book in the class library or make it available for class check out.

"Here's our tree," Dad says. It has been our tree forever and ever.
Mom says I should spread the blanket so we can sit and admire our tree.
"Look," he whispers. We stop. A deer is watching us.
We sing "Oh Come, all ye Faithful," and "Old MacDonald Had a Farm."
I lie in bed and think of our tree and the animals having Christmas dinner around it.
We scatter shelled nuts and bread crumbs and pieces of apple.
On the night before Christmas we always go to find our tree.
An owl hoots, deep in the darkness.
"Can I put on the popcorn chain?" Nina asks.

8

Color the Tree

In the *Night Tree* the family left lots of food under the tree. Check the color code below and color each bulb and part of the tree the correct color.

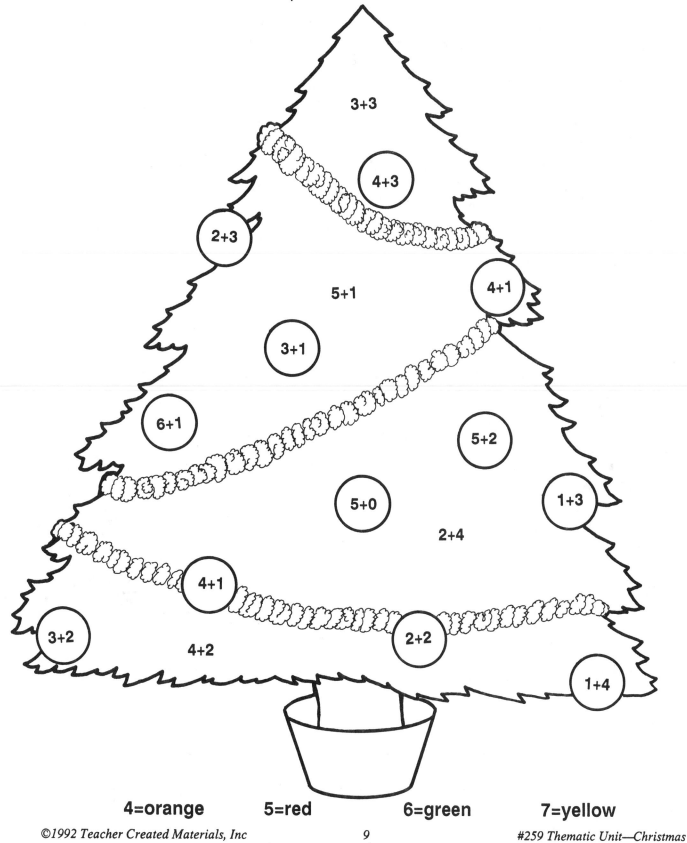

4=orange   **5=red**   **6=green**   **7=yellow**

Tagging Christmas Trees

Information: You will need to locate where Christmas trees sold in your state come from originally. This can be done by calling a local nursery that sells Christmas trees. If there are Christmas tree farms in your area, contact them and arrange a field trip. Find out if they will allow you to bring tags to attach to the trees to trace where the trees are sold. If there are no tree farms in your area, see the activity entitled "Where Do Christmas Trees Come From?" (page 11)

Materials: 3" X 5" index cards (green, if available), thin wire, hole punch, pencils, crayons, rubber stamp with school name & address (optional), map of North America on pages 13-14 and\or globe.

Directions: Discuss where Christmas trees come from in your area. Point out these areas on the map or the globe. Tell the children about the field trip to a Christmas tree farm. Guide them to figure out how they can find out where all the trees are sold. If no one mentions tagging the trees, present the idea.

Discuss what should be written on the tags and let them dictate to you. You can write the dictation on the chalkboard or on chart paper. Copy or type the note and reproduce it. Be sure it will fit on the 3" X 5" cards. The children will cut and paste the note on each card. The school name and address needs to be written or stamped on the other side of the card. Letting the children practice addressing the card to the school is an excellent way to get children to learn how to write addresses. Your tag might read like this:

Please tell us who you are and what city and state you live in. We want to find out where this tree was shipped and locate you on our school map. Please mail this card back to us. Thank you.

_____

Name

_____

City and State

When the notes are completed with the message on one side and the school address on the other side, punch a hole in one side of the note and attach a wire loop to the hole. Twist or tie the wire to secure it to the note.

When the notes come back, mark the area on the North American map with push pins or tags telling the address. Write a thank you note to the tree farm and let them know where the notes came from.

Where Do Christmas Trees Come From?

Find out where the Christmas trees in your area come from. Find out something about that area's agricultural products and general information about the state.

Materials: large map of North America and\or globe; copies of the map on page 13-14 and the questionnaire on page 12; crayons or marking pens

Directions: Discuss where the Christmas trees available in your area come from. Find out other information about the area. Give each child a map of North America and have them trace a line from their home to where the trees came from. Draw a picture of the product on the map. Answer the questionnaire on page 12 either individually or as a class.

Extension: 1. Investigate your own area to find a manufactured or agricultural product that is shipped to some other area of the country. Use the maps on page 13-14 to trace the product. Find out how the product is shipped.

2. Visit a factory or farm in your area to learn more about their products.

3. Make a list of words used during this study.

4. Describe the climate in areas where the product is shipped.

Night Tree

Where Do Christmas Trees Come From? *(cont.)*

Use with map on pages 13-14.

Draw a picture of your Christmas tree in this box.

1. What states or provinces do your Christmas trees come from? Write the answer here and draw lines on the map showing the route they might take to get to your state.

_____

2. What states or provinces do the trees have to cross to get to your state?

_____

_____

3. Do you think the trees are sent by car, bus, train, truck, or boat?

_____

4. How many days ago do you think the trees were cut?

_____

5. How many days do you think it will take the tree to drop all its needles or to turn brown?

_____

Map of North America

Map of North America *(cont.)*

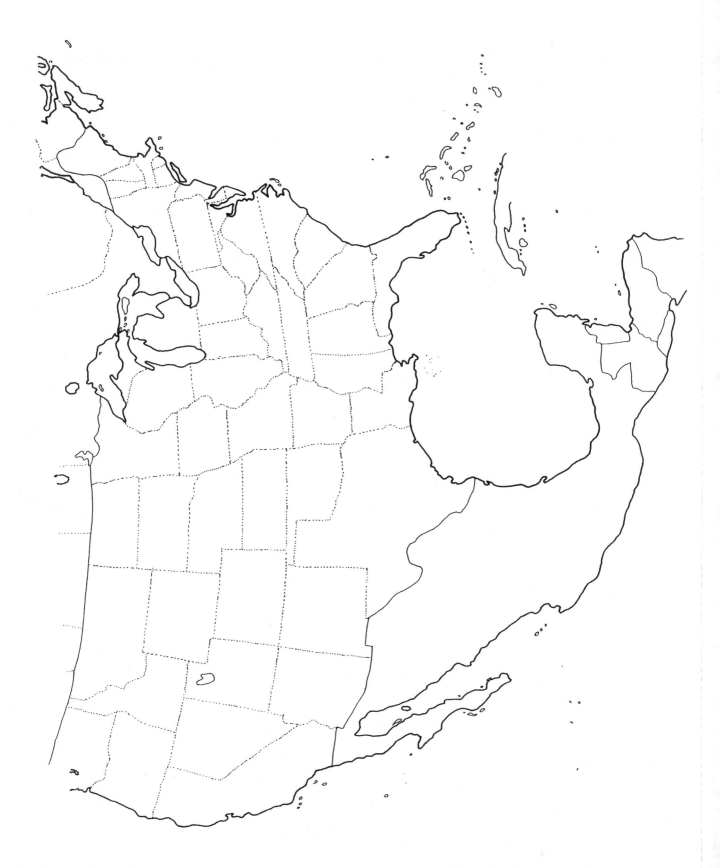

Stand Up Christmas Tree

Preparation: Copy tree pattern on tagboard for children to trace around. Cut out.

Materials: tagboard patterns; green construction paper; stapler; glitter; oil crayons; small colored buttons (optional)

Directions: Trace around the tree pattern on two sheets of green paper. Cut out both trees. Fold one tree in half vertically. Staple it to the flat tree with the folded half sticking out. The tree will stand up. Decorate the tree with glitter, oil crayons and button ornaments.

Writing Ideas

Pretend this is the tree the family decorated in *Night Tree*. What animals will come to visit it? How old do you think this tree is? Would you cut it down? If you had a favorite tree in the forest that you decorated for the animals, what food would you use?

History of Christmas Trees

No one knows for sure how the custom of bringing trees into our homes at Christmas time started. We know that during the 1500's German people decorated trees in their homes. These early trees were decorated with homemade paper objects and lots of food to eat. Often fresh apples, cookies and candies were hung on the tree. Special small candles were hung on the branches. Beautiful glass ornaments were made in Germany and helped decorate the trees. When the Germans settled in America they brought the Christmas tree tradition with them. In 1856, President Franklin Pierce set up the first White House Christmas tree. Since then people in the United States have brought trees into their homes at Christmas time.

15

Popcorn Christmas Trees

Materials: pointed ice cream cones (one per child); 2 cans of white frosting; green food coloring; craft sticks; small paper cups or containers; popped pop corn; red cinnamon candies or other small candies to stick on tree for decoration; paper sticker stars; toothpicks; mixing spoon; wax paper (optional)

Teacher Directions: Open cans of frosting and mix with green food coloring. Stir until color is blended into the frosting. Put a small amount of frosting on wax paper or in small cups for every two children. Each child will need one craft stick, one cone, frosting, popcorn, paper stars, toothpick, and a few red candies.

Directions: Using the craft sticks, spread frosting on one side of the cone. Immediately press popcorn into the frosting. Continue spreading on frosting and pressing in popcorn until all sides are covered. Decorate with red candies that have been dipped in frosting. Stick the paper stars to a toothpick and gently insert the toothpick into the top of the tree.

Extensions:

1. How did you make this popcorn tree? Write down all the steps.

2. Draw a picture of your tree.

3. Decide whether you want to take your tree home or eat it!

4. Make a popcorn Christmas tree for the birds. Instead of using frosting and red candies, use frosting and bird seed to decorate the tree.

The Wild Christmas Reindeer

by Jan Brett

Summary

It is Teeka's task to find and train the wild reindeer to drive Santa's sleigh. She has never done this before and decides that being very firm and loud is the way to get the reindeer trained. To her dismay, the reindeer become more unmanageable each day. Children delight in hearing and seeing how Teeka solves her problem in this beautifully illustrated story.

The outline below is a suggested plan for using the various activities presented in this unit. You may adapt the ideas to meet specific needs in your classroom.

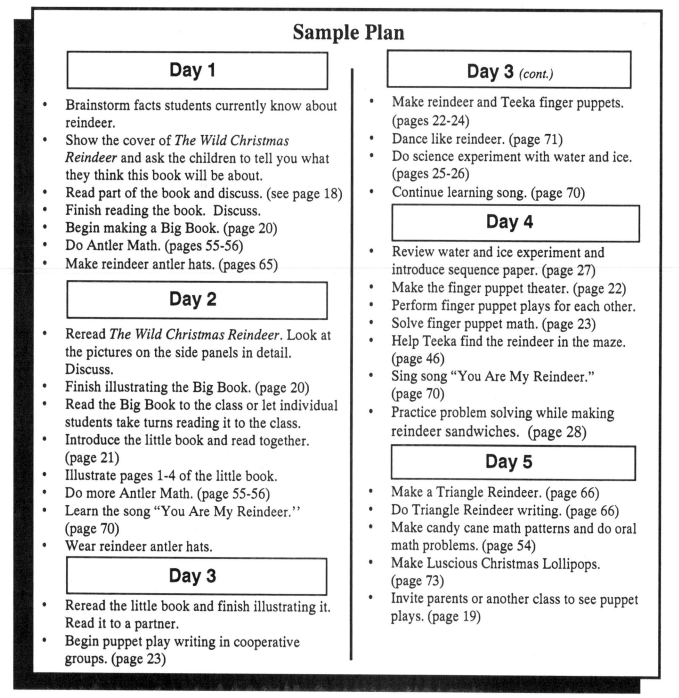

Sample Plan

Day 1

- Brainstorm facts students currently know about reindeer.
- Show the cover of *The Wild Christmas Reindeer* and ask the children to tell you what they think this book will be about.
- Read part of the book and discuss. (see page 18)
- Finish reading the book. Discuss.
- Begin making a Big Book. (page 20)
- Do Antler Math. (pages 55-56)
- Make reindeer antler hats. (pages 65)

Day 2

- Reread *The Wild Christmas Reindeer*. Look at the pictures on the side panels in detail. Discuss.
- Finish illustrating the Big Book. (page 20)
- Read the Big Book to the class or let individual students take turns reading it to the class.
- Introduce the little book and read together. (page 21)
- Illustrate pages 1-4 of the little book.
- Do more Antler Math. (page 55-56)
- Learn the song "You Are My Reindeer." (page 70)
- Wear reindeer antler hats.

Day 3

- Reread the little book and finish illustrating it. Read it to a partner.
- Begin puppet play writing in cooperative groups. (page 23)

Day 3 (cont.)

- Make reindeer and Teeka finger puppets. (pages 22-24)
- Dance like reindeer. (page 71)
- Do science experiment with water and ice. (pages 25-26)
- Continue learning song. (page 70)

Day 4

- Review water and ice experiment and introduce sequence paper. (page 27)
- Make the finger puppet theater. (page 22)
- Perform finger puppet plays for each other.
- Solve finger puppet math. (page 23)
- Help Teeka find the reindeer in the maze. (page 46)
- Sing song "You Are My Reindeer." (page 70)
- Practice problem solving while making reindeer sandwiches. (page 28)

Day 5

- Make a Triangle Reindeer. (page 66)
- Do Triangle Reindeer writing. (page 66)
- Make candy cane math patterns and do oral math problems. (page 54)
- Make Luscious Christmas Lollipops. (page 73)
- Invite parents or another class to see puppet plays. (page 19)

Overview of Activities

Setting the Stage

1. Gather books and pictures about reindeer for display. Discuss reindeer and where they live. How do they differ from the deer in North America?

2. Brainstorm with the children and create a web entitled, "Facts we know about reindeer." Have them give all the facts they know and write them down on the web. Write down any questions they might have.

3. Discuss reality versus fiction. Do reindeer really fly? Why not?

Enjoying the Book

1. Show the reindeer on the cover of the book and discuss the look in their eyes.

2. Read the book until you finish the page where the reindeer horns are completely tangled. Ask the children to tell you what they would do if they were Teeka.

3. Finish reading the book. Discuss how and why Teeka changed. Have students ever had similar experiences? If you want someone to do something for you, how should you ask them?

4. Discuss manners. Practice asking classmates for help. Role play this with partners.

5. Dramatize the story with one child being Teeka and eight children as reindeer. In the beginning of the story Teeka is very rough with the reindeer. At the end of the story she has changed her approach. Dramatize again with a partner. Take turns being Teeka and the reindeer. Discuss how it felt to be yelled at by Teeka.

6. Look at all the pictures on the side panels in the book. Discuss all the presents the elves are making. Pick one present you would like to receive and draw a picture of it. Write a sentence about the present that tells why you would like it.

18

Overview of Activities *(cont.)*

Extending the Book

1. Invite another class over and read the book to them. Dramatize the book for them with one child as Teeka and eight children wearing their reindeer antler hats as reindeer. (page 65)

2. Have each child in your room find a partner from the other class. Decide who will be the reindeer and who will be Teeka. Dramatize how Teeka changes her behavior toward the reindeer.

3. Plan to present the puppet play to parents and or to another class. Write invitations inviting people to come to the play. The invitations might look like this:

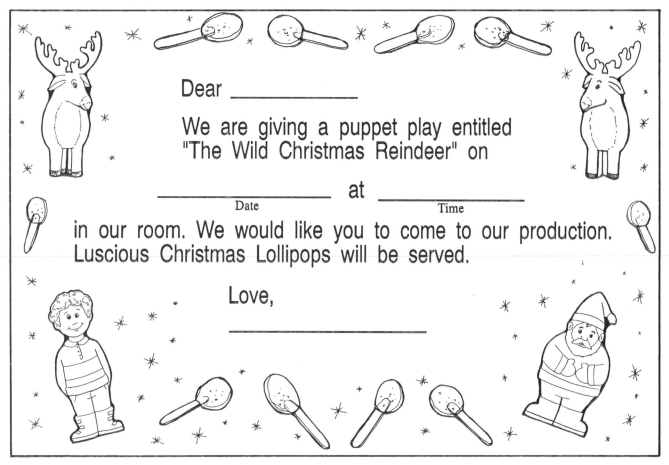

Dear _____

We are giving a puppet play entitled "The Wild Christmas Reindeer" on

_____ at _____
      Date   Time

in our room. We would like you to come to our production. Luscious Christmas Lollipops will be served.

Love,

_____

4. Make Luscious Christmas Lollipops to serve at the performance. (page 73)

5. Divide the audience into small groups to watch different groups of children giving their puppet plays. Several puppet plays will be going on at the same time.

6. Demonstrate puppet math with the children using their puppets and theaters for the parents or guests. (page 22-23)

7. Pass out Luscious Christmas Lollipops and start a lollipop story. Include your guests in the story telling. (page 73)

Book Making

Big Books

Materials: 11 pieces of 12" X 18" white or light colored construction paper; markers; crayons; tempera paint

Directions: Reread the book. Discuss what happened when Teeka first tried to train the reindeer. Make a Big Book by discussing with the children what happened in the story and the order of each event. Use text similar to the little book on page 21. Write one event on each page. Organize the children in groups of two or three and let them illustrate the eight pages of text. They will also need one page for the cover, a page at the end of the book saying "The End" and a page for all the illustrators to sign their names.

Little Books

Materials: One copy of the little book (page 21) for each student; crayons

Preparation:

1. Fold page 21 in half lengthwise after cutting along outside lines.

2. Fold in half again.

3. Fold in half again.

4. Unfold the paper. (You should have eight parts now.)

5. Fold in half widthwise.

6. Cut or tear along the center crease from the folded edge to the dot. (See diagram below.)

7. Open the paper.

8. Fold it lengthwise again.

9. Push the end sections together to fold into a little book. Four pages will be formed.

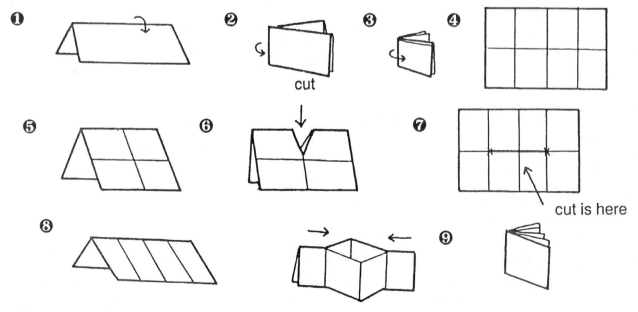

Little Book

Teeka shouts, "Move, Move, Move!" The reindeer are upset. Teeka brushes their fur too hard and their ears turn pink.

She goes to the tundra and finds Bramble, Heather, Windswept, Lichen, Snowball, Crag, Twilight, and Tundra.

When Teeka yells and tries to get them to stand in two lines, the reindeer fight.

Teeka's job is to train the wild reindeer for Santa.

Teeka realizes she must be gentle with the reindeer. She speaks to them gently and they listen. They are easy to train now.

The Wild Christmas Reindeer

Teeka watches with joy as the trained reindeer carry Santa's sleigh into the night.

The End

Finger Puppets
How to Make Finger Puppets

Materials: patterns on page 24, tagboard; white and several other colors of construction paper; scissors; crayons or oil crayons; glue or staples

Preparation: Using the patterns on page 24, cut out tagboard models for the children to trace.

Directions:

1. Have the children trace and cut out the reindeer and Teeka patterns on construction paper.
2. Add antlers for the reindeer and make clothes for Teeka by coloring or cutting them out of construction paper and gluing onto the figures.
3. Color in features using crayons or oil crayons.
4. Cut a small rectangular piece of construction paper 3" X 1". Make a cylinder with it and glue the 1" ends together. Hold the ends and count to ten so they will dry completely.
5. Glue the ring on the back of the puppet and count to ten again.
6. Fit your finger in the ring. You have a finger puppet!

Puppet Theater

Materials: shoe box with lid, tempera paints, scissors, glitter, glue, construction paper or railroad board, fabric scraps (optional)

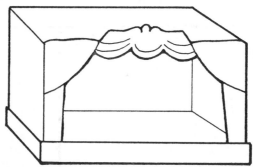

Directions:

1. Cut a long rectangle in the front of the lid. Cut the rectangle one inch wide and the length of your lid. The lid with its opening will be the theater floor.
2. Glue the uncut side of the lid to the long side of the box.
3. Add a construction paper or railroad board facade to the top of the box for the stage.
4. Paint the inside and the outside of the box.
5. Add fabric curtains or paper curtains to the sides of the stage.
6. Use glitter to decorate the facade and curtains, if desired.

   To use your puppet theater set it on a table or desk with the edge of the box hanging over the edge of the desk or set the puppet theater on another smaller box. The puppets will come up through the slit in the box lid.

Variations:

1. Craft stick puppets work well with this stage, too.
2. If you don't have time to make a puppet stage, just use the edge of a table or desk as the puppet stage. Cover it with a sheet or towel.

Finger Puppets *(cont.)*

Writing a Puppet Play

Reread *The Wild Christmas Reindeer*. Discuss writing a play. Which characters do students want to use in the play? Discuss the use of colons and the proper format for writing a play.

Play writing can be a group activity, with the teacher writing the parts of the play on the chalkboard and children copying their own parts, or it can be a cooperative group activity for older children.

If you are using cooperative groups, organize children in groups of four. Let each group make their own version of the play. When all groups are ready to present their plays, team up 2 to 3 groups together. The groups will give their plays for these larger groups and then rotate until all groups have had an opportunity to see and give all productions.

Variations:

1. Let children make up their own version of the book or make up an entirely new play using characters from the story or new characters which they have made.

2. Add a train, a boy, and Santa Claus and act out *The Polar Express*.

Finger Puppet Math

Materials: finger puppets (page 24); puppet theater (page 22); chalk; chalkboard; and erasers or paper and pencil

Directions: Each child should have chalk and a chalkboard or pencil and paper. The teacher gathers up several of the puppets and a puppet stage and begins to tell story problems with them.

For Example:

"Once upon a time, Bramble and Heather Reindeer went for a walk. (Show two reindeer on the stage.) *Windswept Reindeer came racing along to join them.* (Bring one more reindeer on stage with them.) *Now there are _____ reindeer."*

The children will write an equation on their chalkboards showing the answer. Continue telling story problems until the children understand how to do it themselves. Form cooperative groups and have students tell stories to each other. One child tells a word problem and the other 2 or 3 children write equations. Let everyone have a turn making up problems and writing the equations.

Variations:

1. Gather all the puppets together and have the children estimate how many there are altogether.

2. Gather all the puppets together and count them by 2's, 3's, 4's and 5's.

Finger Puppet Patterns

Water and Ice

Information: Water exists in three states: as a liquid, a solid, and a gas. In this lesson, we will demonstrate the liquid and solid states of water. Water (the liquid state) changes to ice (the solid state) when the temperature drops below 32 degrees F (0 degrees C). The ice melts when the temperature rises above 32 degrees. Water and ice can change back and forth, depending on the temperature.

Materials: four ice cubes; four styrofoam trays; numbers 1-4 written on four index cards; timer or alarm clock; copies of the form on **page 26** for each child, pencils

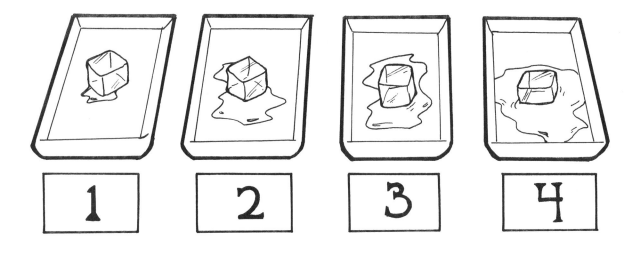

Directions: "Teeka and the reindeer live in a land of ice and snow. How long do you think it would take all that ice to melt? Let's do some experimenting with ice cubes to find out how long they take to melt." Number the trays 1-4. Place the ice cubes on trays in various parts of the classroom. Place a number card over or beside each tray. Put one tray in the window, one tray near the heating vents, one tray on a desk, and another tray in a place of your choosing. Set a timer or alarm clock for 15 minutes.

Using the form on page 26 have the children fill out their own estimations of how many minutes it will take to melt each ice cube. Will they all melt at the same time? If they melt at different times, why does this happen?

Introduce the terms liquid and solid. Is ice a solid or a liquid? Give examples of each. (i.e., water, milk, juice versus ice, ice cream)

Extension:

1. Do Sequence page 27. What are the steps that happen when water goes from a liquid to a solid?

2. Experiment with ice cream in the trays. What will happen?

3. Research what life is like in very cold regions of the world.

4. Investigate icebergs and glaciers.

5. Find out what winter sports people play in cold climates.

Water and Ice *(cont.)*

(Use with page 25)

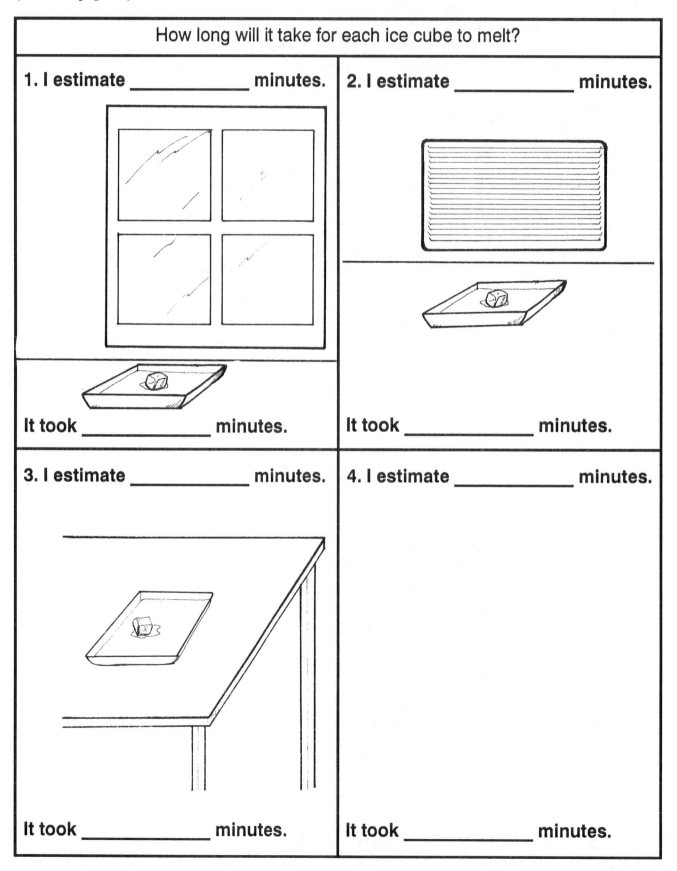

How long will it take for each ice cube to melt?

1. I estimate _____ minutes.

It took _____ minutes.

2. I estimate _____ minutes.

It took _____ minutes.

3. I estimate _____ minutes.

It took _____ minutes.

4. I estimate _____ minutes.

It took _____ minutes.

26

How Does Water Change To Ice?

Put these pictures in the correct order on 5 ½" X 10" construction paper.

Reindeer Sandwiches

Materials: 4" X 5" white or beige paper (at least two pieces per student); scissors; rulers; ingredients below; spoons or craft sticks; small containers to hold ingredients; paring knife

Ingredients: whole wheat bread; peanut butter; raisins; red apple slices; pretzel sticks

Directions: Give each child a piece of 4" X 5" piece of paper. Ask them to figure out how they will divide it to make 4 triangles. Let them experiment. Do not show them how to do this. Allow plenty of time and give them more paper, if needed. When they have solved the problem, let them cut their slice of bread in the same way. Spread peanut butter on two of the triangles. Decorate with raisins for eyes, a slice of red apple for the nose, and pretzels for the antlers. Each child can eat two triangles. Extra bread may be saved for another day's snack or fed to the birds.

Extensions:

1. Draw a picture of your reindeer sandwich.

2. Write about your reindeer sandwich. If you make another one, will you make it the same or will you change it? What do you think your reindeer would say if it could talk to you? Would he run away like the Gingerbread Boy? Does your reindeer have a name?

The Polar Express

by Chris Van Allsburg

Summary

On Christmas Eve a boy is taken on a mysterious train to the North Pole. The trip to the pole is a glorious experience through dark forests and high mountains. When he arrives, Santa chooses him to be the child that receives the first gift of Christmas. He asks for and receives one bell from the harness of the reindeer. It is with great sadness that he discovers he has lost the bell on the way home. At home he finds the bell again, and learns a special secret about it. The illustrations in this book are exquisite. This book has become a classic Christmas book for children of all ages.

The outline below is a suggested plan for using the various activities presented in this unit. You may adapt the ideas to meet specific needs in your classroom.

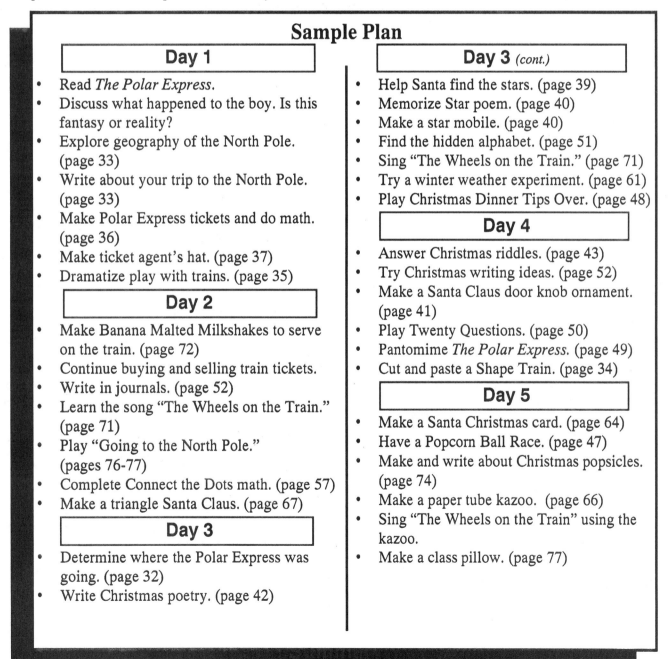

Sample Plan

Day 1

- Read *The Polar Express*.
- Discuss what happened to the boy. Is this fantasy or reality?
- Explore geography of the North Pole. (page 33)
- Write about your trip to the North Pole. (page 33)
- Make Polar Express tickets and do math. (page 36)
- Make ticket agent's hat. (page 37)
- Dramatize play with trains. (page 35)

Day 2

- Make Banana Malted Milkshakes to serve on the train. (page 72)
- Continue buying and selling train tickets.
- Write in journals. (page 52)
- Learn the song "The Wheels on the Train." (page 71)
- Play "Going to the North Pole." (pages 76-77)
- Complete Connect the Dots math. (page 57)
- Make a triangle Santa Claus. (page 67)

Day 3

- Determine where the Polar Express was going. (page 32)
- Write Christmas poetry. (page 42)

Day 3 (cont.)

- Help Santa find the stars. (page 39)
- Memorize Star poem. (page 40)
- Make a star mobile. (page 40)
- Find the hidden alphabet. (page 51)
- Sing "The Wheels on the Train." (page 71)
- Try a winter weather experiment. (page 61)
- Play Christmas Dinner Tips Over. (page 48)

Day 4

- Answer Christmas riddles. (page 43)
- Try Christmas writing ideas. (page 52)
- Make a Santa Claus door knob ornament. (page 41)
- Play Twenty Questions. (page 50)
- Pantomime *The Polar Express*. (page 49)
- Cut and paste a Shape Train. (page 34)

Day 5

- Make a Santa Christmas card. (page 64)
- Have a Popcorn Ball Race. (page 47)
- Make and write about Christmas popsicles. (page 74)
- Make a paper tube kazoo. (page 66)
- Sing "The Wheels on the Train" using the kazoo.
- Make a class pillow. (page 77)

Overview of Activities

Setting the Stage

1. Find books about trains, winter weather, and the North Pole from the library. Post pictures of early trains on a bulletin board.

2. Using a large appliance box, let the children make a train by painting the sides and cutting out one side. Or get small boxes and let children make individual train cars that they can wear. Let them form a train and parade around the classroom.

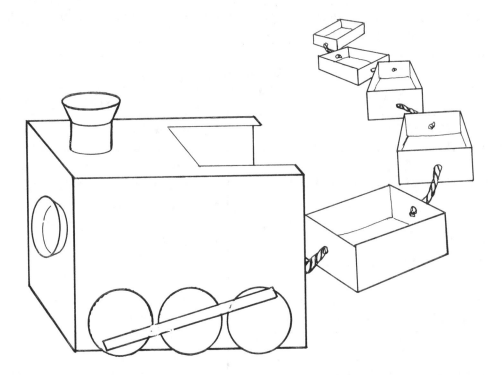

3. Plan a field trip on a local train. Call your travel agent to make reservations.

Enjoying the Book

1. Read the book. Look carefully at the illustrations. What is the weather like in many of the pictures?

2. Can we make pictures that look like it's snowing? Discuss. Have the children paint or color a picture and spatter white paint on the drawing. To add spatter paint, place the completed painting in the bottom of a box. Dip a small brush or an old toothbrush in white paint and gently flick white on the painting to make the illusion of snow.

3. Reread the last two pages of the book. Discuss why the bell rings. What does the author mean? Hide bells around the classroom and let children find and ring them.

4. Ring a bell at various times and in different locations around the classroom. When the children hear the bell ringing, they signal you.

Overview of Activities *(cont.)*

Enjoying the Book *(cont.)*

5. Ask the children to bring bells from home. Put them in a sound center and let the children listen to the different sounds as they ring the bells.

6. Try experiments with sound. Take a string three feet long and tie a metal spoon in the center of it. Hold the ends of the string to your ears. Swing the spoon back and forth several times. Do you hear a sound? (They should not be able to.) Now, swing the spoon until it hits the end of your desk. Do you hear a sound? (They should hear a sound like a church bell.) You made the spoon vibrate. The vibrations travel along the string to your ears. Try a fork or a bigger spoon. Does the sound change? Place these items in the sound center for children to continue experimenting with.

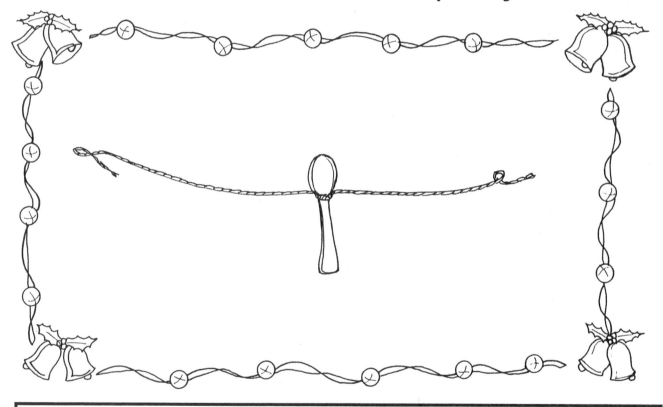

Extending the Book

1. Read the riddles on page 43. Let students try writing their own Christmas riddles. Illustrate the riddles on separate pieces of paper and match up the riddle with the picture. Place on a bulletin board.

2. Make Christmas placemats to use on the train trip on the Polar Express (page 68). Have students take them home to use for Christmas dinner or make them as presents for their families.

3. Let each child make a big triangle Santa Claus (page 67). Hang them up like mobiles around your room. Or make a snowy North Pole background and place them on the background to make a mural.

4. Find pictures of different types of trains. Compare them to the Polar Express. What type of energy do they run on?

Where Was the Polar Express Going?

1. Find the smoke puff's message.

2. Color.

‾‾‾‾ ‾‾‾‾ ‾‾‾‾ ‾‾‾‾ ‾‾‾‾ ‾‾‾‾ ‾‾‾‾ ‾‾‾‾
 6   4   2   8   7   1   6   4

‾‾‾‾ ‾‾‾‾ ‾‾‾‾ ‾‾‾‾!
 3   7   5   2

Challenge: Make up your own secret code to exchange messages with a friend.

Trip to the North Pole

Geography

If the Polar Express picked us up at our school, what route would it take to get us to the North Pole?

Materials: map on pages 13-14; train below on this page; scissors; crayons

Directions: Give each child a map and the train below to cut out and color. Trace the route from where you live to the North Pole using the train. Trace over the route with a crayon. Ask the following questions: What countries would you have to cross? Could a train go all that way? Would we need other means of transportation? How long do you think the trip would take?

Writing

Preparation: Make a journal for each child by binding or stapling 15-20 sheets of typing paper together. A construction paper cover can be added on the front and the back of the book.

Directions: Choose a topic and write about it in your journal. (Each of these questions could provide one day's writing assignment for a child.) After writing, have children illustrate their stories and read them to partners.

- What do you see when you look out the window?

- What are they serving to eat and drink on the train?

- Who is with you on this train?

- Will you see Santa?

- How would you feel if you were the child chosen to get the first present?

- If you are the child that gets the first gift, what will you ask for?

Shape Train

Cut out these shapes and glue on dotted lines to make a train.

Challenge: Try to make the train shape without using the outline. Glue to construction paper.

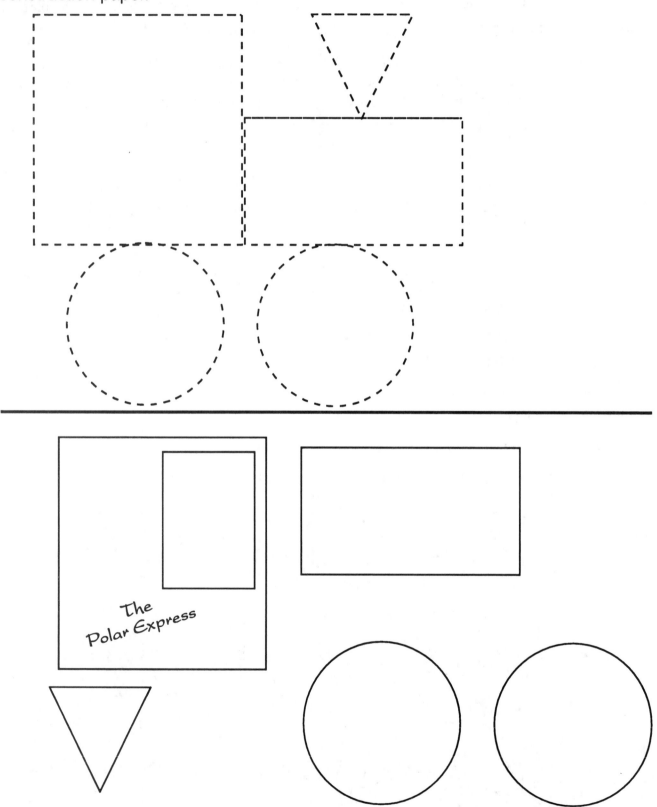

The
Polar Express

Train Station

Build a train station. Role play buying tickets and riding on the train.

Materials: Page 36 for tickets; real pennies or paper pennies on page 38; envelopes or containers to hold pennies; butcher paper for railroad station sign; construction paper for price sign; ticket agent hat on page 37; colored pencils or markers

Directions: Have each child make several tickets. They should be only two different prices, one for adults and one for children. Let the class decide what the prices should be. For younger children, prices under 5¢ would be best. Older children could use higher prices. Vote on a name for your train station and write it on butcher paper. Let the children decorate with colored pencils or markers and hang it up over the area you plan to use for the train station.

Two children will need to be the ticket agents. They can wear the hats made from the pattern on page 37. All children can make a hat and when it's their turn to be the ticket agents they can wear their own hats. One child will be in charge of collecting the money and making sure he\she is paid the correct amount for the tickets. The other person will be in charge of returning pennies to the containers (10 to a container) so other children can continue to buy tickets.

Tickets Please

The boy in *The Polar Express* doesn't seem to need a ticket to get on the train. If we were to go on a train, would we need a ticket?

Preparation: Make your own tickets or make copies of the tickets below.

Materials: copies of tickets below (at least two per student); pencils; pennies (real or use pennies on page 38)

Directions: Let the children fill in their names and the cost of the ticket. For young children keep the cost below 5¢. Older children can work with nickels and dimes and charge more for the tickets.

After the children have filled out the tickets with their names and the price, they will need to place the appropriate number of pennies on their tickets. Find a partner and check each other's prices and pennies. Trade tickets and "buy" your partner's. Trade with another child and "buy" that ticket. See page 35 for directions on setting up a train station.

Polar Express Ticket	Polar Express Ticket	Polar Express Ticket
Admit **1**	Admit **1**	Admit **1**
Polar Express Ticket — This is a ticket to the North Pole. Only those children that truly believe in the magic of Christmas will be able to go on this special train. I, _____ believe in the magic of Christmas. This ticket costs _____	**Polar Express Ticket** — This is a ticket to the North Pole. Only those children that truly believe in the magic of Christmas will be able to go on this special train. I, _____ believe in the magic of Christmas. This ticket costs _____	**Polar Express Ticket** — This is a ticket to the North Pole. Only those children that truly believe in the magic of Christmas will be able to go on this special train. I, _____ believe in the magic of Christmas. This ticket costs _____

Ticket Agent Hat

Directions: Attach to 2" x 24" piece of construction paper. Adjust to fit child's head.

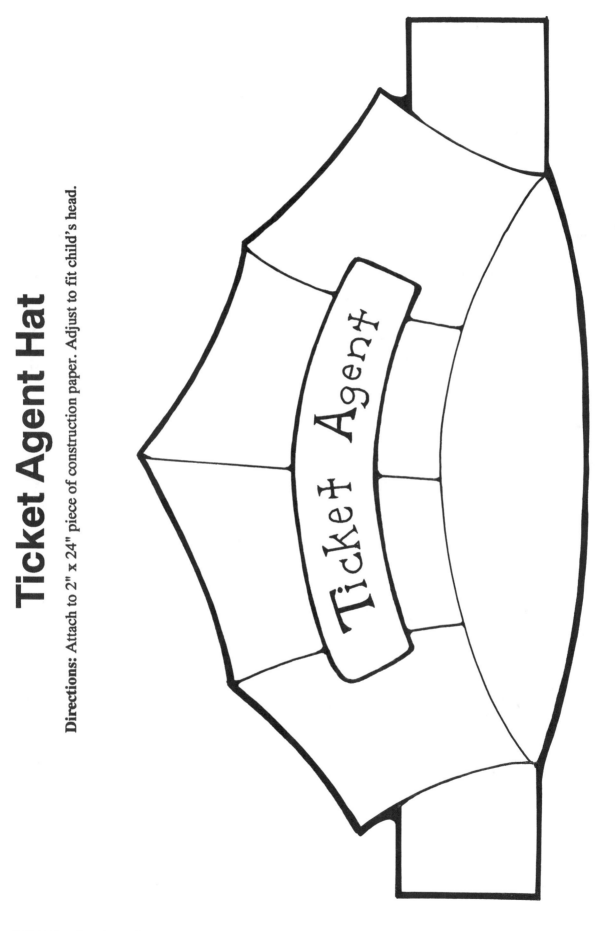

Ticket Agent

Pennies

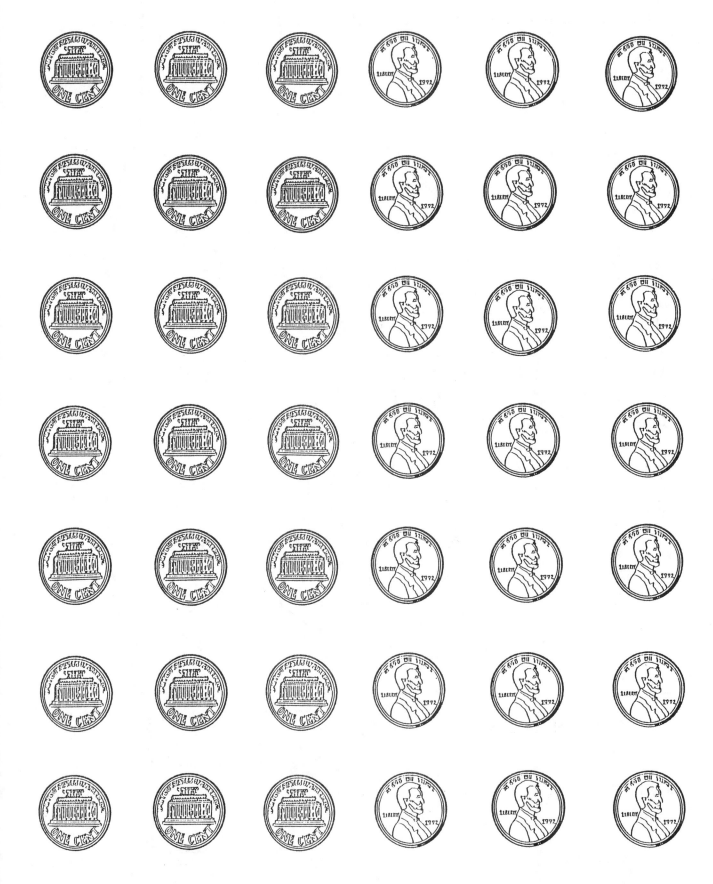

Help Santa

Santa looks to the stars to help him navigate around the world. Help him find the constellations by connecting the numbers.

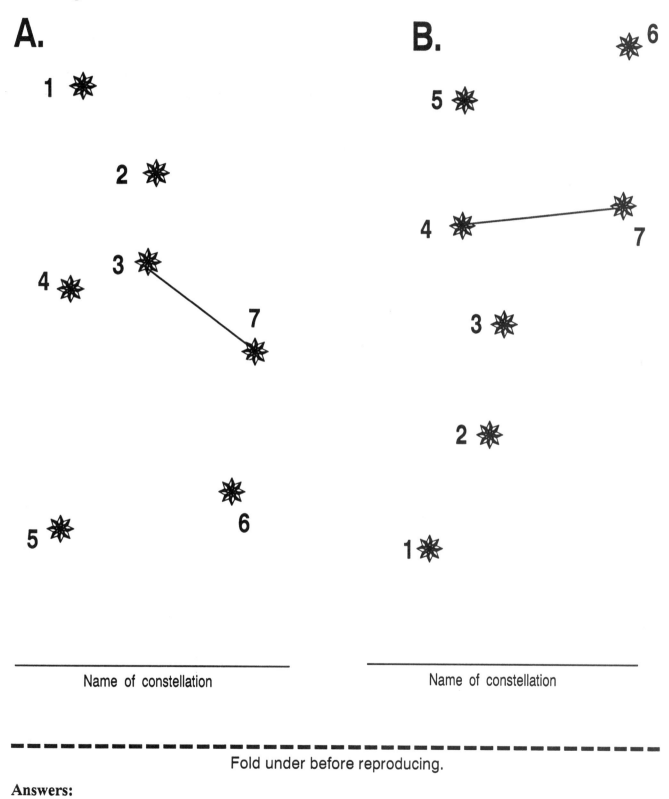

Name of constellation

Name of constellation

Answers:

A. Big Dipper

B. Little Dipper

Star Mobile

Materials: clear plastic gallon milk jugs; yarn or string; construction paper or tagboard; crayons; glitter; glue; hole punch; scissors

Directions: Cut the milk jug in half, saving the top half for the mobile. Recycle the bottom half. Punch holes along the bottom edge. Cut various shapes and sizes of stars out of construction paper or tagboard. Color and add glitter to front and back of each star. Punch a hole at both ends of each shape. Attach the shapes with string or yarn to the milk carton. Attach a string to the top and hang your star mobile up to admire.

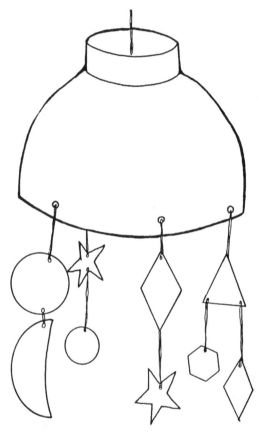

Extensions: String the stars in the shape of a constellation. Write the name of the constellation on the top of the milk jug with a permanent marker. Write in your journal how you made your star mobile. Go outside at night and try to find your constellation. Learn the following poem:

Star light

Star bright

First star I see tonight

Wish I may

Wish I might

Have the wish I wish tonight.

Write the poem on chart paper and help the children memorize it. This poem could be printed in Big or Little Books, too.

Santa Claus Door Knob Ornament

Materials: pattern on this page copied on red construction paper; scissors; black crayon; white crayon or white chalk; white cotton balls (1 per student)

Directions: Decorate the Santa Claus with white chalk or white crayon and black crayon. Cut out the figure by cutting up through the center and cutting out the circle. This is the part that will fit over the door knob. Add a cotton ball on the top of Santa's hat. Children love to hang this on a door knob and look at it!

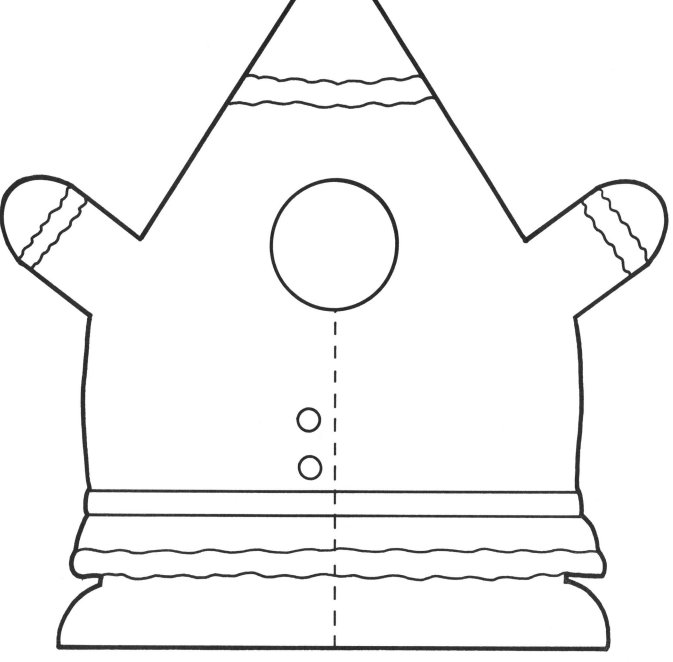

Christmas Couplets

Information: A couplet is a two line poem that rhymes. i.e.

Christmas green, Christmas red,

By Santa Claus, reindeer were led.

To write a Christmas couplet, use the word Christmas twice in the first line. The word Christmas should be followed by a color word. The second line must rhyme with the first line. Let the children practice saying couplets with you and thinking of rhyming words to use. When they have made up some, write several on the chalkboard or on chart paper. Have the children write their own couplets in the Santa Pop-Up card on **page 69** or make another Christmas card and decorate it. Or, write the couplets and place them in a special class book.

Let the children pick any Christmas theme and write couplets to go with the theme.

Try writing reindeer or tree couplets.

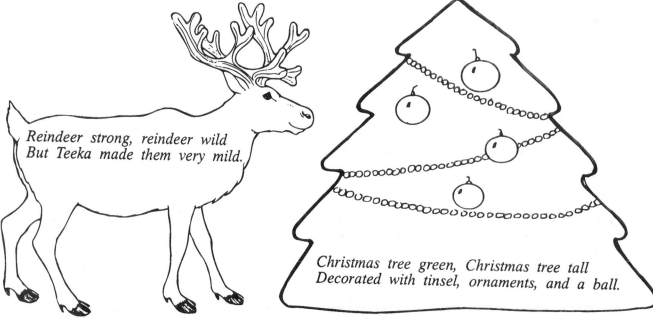

Christmas Riddles

Read and discuss this paper together. Fill in the blanks. Try writing a riddle of your own.

Four hooves
That pound the sky.
Long branches on
My head do lie.
Who am I?

_____

Bulbs and ornaments
Angels and light,
Presents at my feet
Christmas night.
What am I?

_____

My beard is white, my suit is red,
I have a pointed cap upon my head.
I bring presents in the night,
To make your life a great delight.
Who am I?

_____

Bright colors, red and green
The best wrappings we've ever seen.
Lots of ribbons, pretty bows
Inside this, only Santa knows.
What am I?

_____

Ding Dong, Ding Dong, I do say,
As I ring on Christmas day.
Listen carefully you will hear
Sounds that are so very dear.
What am I?

_____

Red and white,
Curved at the top.
I'm so sweet
I can't be beat.
What am I?

_____

- -
(Fold under before reproducing)

Answers: Reindeer, Christmas Tree, Santa, Packages, Bells, Candy Cane

What Do Animals Eat?

Materials: paper or journals; tagboard strips; crayons or markers; chalk, chalkboard or overhead projector

Directions: Reread *Night Tree*. Discuss and list on the chalkboard or overhead projector all the food items that the family made for the animals. Beside each food, list the animal or animals that might eat that item.

Food	Animal
popcorn	birds
sunflower seeds	birds
apples	raccoon, skunk, bear

Using the list, have each child write sentences about the story. For example: The robin is eating the popcorn. A skunk likes the apples.

Assign partners. Read your sentences to your partner. Copy these sentences on tagboard strips and let the children illustrate their strips. (For example, over the word skunk, draw a skunk and over the apple, draw an apple.) Use these sentence strips in a pocket chart or place around the room or on a bulletin board for the children to read.

Birds eat seeds.

Racoons eat apples.

Extensions: Which animals live in your area? What could you do for the animals in your area to make sure they have a happy Christmas? Write a sentence about what you plan to do to help feed the animals. Illustrate the sentence or sentences and place them on the bulletin board. Or, make all the pages into a class book.

Place the Ornaments

  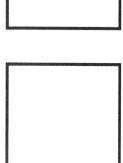

Cut and glue here ornaments that are up **high** on the tree.

Cut and glue here ornaments that are in the **middle** of the tree.

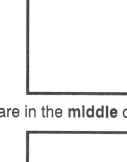 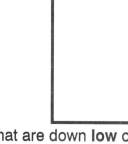

Cut and glue here ornaments that are down **low** on the tree.

- -
cut here

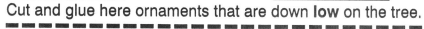 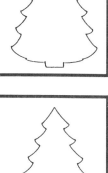 

Help Teeka Find the Wild Reindeer

Connect the letters of the alphabet to lead Teeka to the reindeer.

Popcorn Ball Race

To help the children learn the sound of "P" have a Popcorn Ball Relay Race. Use the extension activities for older children.

Materials: two small white styrofoam balls (these are the "popcorn" balls); two wooden spoons; chalk or string to mark off starting lines for the race

Directions: Choose one child to be the recorder. With young children the teacher may need to do the recording. Divide the class into two teams, by numbering off by two's. Have them hold up the number of fingers after they call out their numbers. Ask team number one to stand on one side of the room and team number two to stand on the other side of the room. Each team is then divided into two parts, facing each other. The first person on each team must roll the "popcorn" ball with a wooden spoon across the room to where the other half of the team is standing. Before he/she gives the ball to a teammate, he/she must shout out a word that begins with "P." Each player should try to use a word no one else has used. The game is won by the side that finishes first.

The teacher or a recorder writes all the "P" words on the chalkboard or on chart paper as the children shout them out. Everyone reads the words when the game is over.

Extensions:

1. Have the children copy the "P" words and make sentences out of them.

2. Alphabetize all the "P" words.

3. Have the teams read the words. Make a game out of it and see which team can finish reading the words first. You will need to time the teams.

4. Use some of the more common words as spelling words and have a spelling review and test.

Christmas Dinner Tips Over

To help children learn to read names of foods and improve listening skills, play the following game.

Materials: chart paper and marking pen or chalk and chalkboard; 2" X 6" strips of white paper; one chair for each child

Directions: Discuss the various foods traditionally eaten at Christmas. Write this list on paper or on the board. Each child chooses which food he/she wants to be for Christmas dinner. If two children choose the same food they must decide between themselves which one will get to be that food and which will need to pick another food. Each child copies the name of his/her food on the 2" X 6" strip of paper and holds it up while playing the game.

Arrange all the chairs in a circle. If you do not have room to do this, divide the class in half and have two games going at once. One child is chosen to be "It." This child calls two names to change places, such as "Roast Beef'' and "Pecan Pie." They must change places immediately while "It" tries to sit in one of their seats. The person left standing is the next "It." At any time "It" may yell "Christmas Dinner Tips Over" and everyone must change places.

Variations:

1. The same name may be given to more than one person. This makes changing places a little more hectic.

2. This same game can be played using the alphabet letters, numbers, vocabulary or spelling words.

48

Pantomime

Directions: Teach the children how to do pantomime using *The Polar Express*. Explain that pantomime is acting without words. Begin the pantomime by acting out the part where the boy hears the train. Continue pantomiming getting on the train, eating candy and drinking hot chocolate, seeing wonderful scenery, meeting Santa, receiving the first gift of Christmas, losing the bell, and finally the joy of finding it again. You will need to demonstrate to the children how to do this. Divide the class into groups of two. One child will do the pantomime and the other will watch. Trade places and repeat. Have the child who is watching guess which incident the other child is depicting.

Extensions:

1. Pantomimists often paint their faces white and wear black clothing. Use white powder or white face paint to paint the children's faces. If you have black clothes available, let them dress up for the role.

2. Write about this activity in journals.

3. Let the children retell the story and write it on chart paper. Cut these sentences into strips and use with a pocket chart or cut up the sentence strips and place them on a long piece of butcher paper. The children can make illustrations above the sentence strips. Have them be sure the sentences are in the correct order before they begin their illustrations.

Christmas Items Twenty Questions

Materials: paper bag or cloth bag containing Christmas pictures cut from old Christmas cards or little toy objects

Directions: One child is "It" and draws an object or picture from the bag, being careful not to let anyone else see the object. Children may only ask questions about the object that can be answered with "yes" or "no." They need to be encouraged to ask about properties or attributes of the object, not the name of the object. Encourage all children to ask questions in complete sentences and answer in complete sentences. After 2-3 minutes of questions and answers, let the children guess the name of the object.

Extension:

1. Each child "keeps" the object they have drawn out of the bag. They return to their desk and write the properties of the object. Or they can record the questions that were asked and the answers given about the object.

2. Use the bag and objects to start a "Round Robin" story. The first child draws an object out of the bag and tells the beginning of a story using that object in the story. When he/she has told as much as he/she wants to, the bag is passed to someone else and they draw an object out and continue the story that was started, using the object that they drew out in their part of the story. For example:

"On Christmas I went to my Grandmother's house. I found this toy under the tree. (Child draws out a toy.) *My grandma told me not to play with it, but to save it for Christmas. But, I wanted to play with it so much, I did anyway. Grandma was not happy. She said......."* The child passes the bag to the next person and lets him/her continue the story using the object he/she will draw out of the bag as the focal point of his/her part of the story.

Find the Hidden Alphabet

Can you find the hidden alphabet? Circle every letter from A to Z.

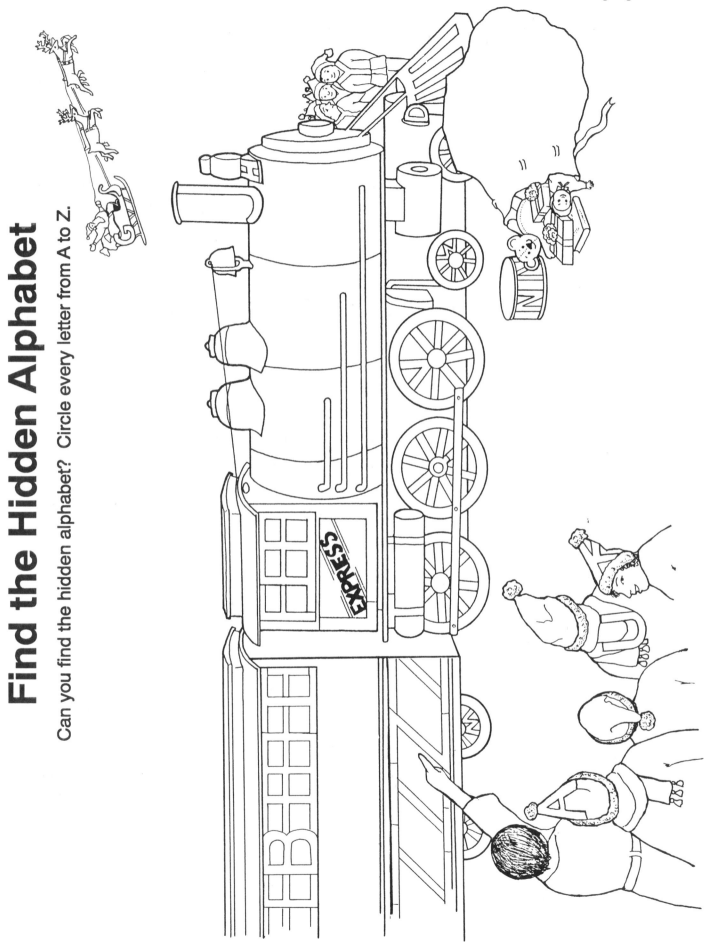

Journal Writing Ideas

Materials: chalkboard; chalk; paper and pencil or journals for students; crayons; scissors; assortment of colored construction paper

Directions: Print one or more of these activities on the board and let children complete the activity.

1. Make a Santa Claus using 2 circles. Add anything else you would like. Make a caption over his head. Write in the caption what you think Santa is saying to you. Post Santa and the caption on the bulletin board.

2. Make a Christmas card. Put an elf in it. Write "Merry Christmas from_____" inside the card.

3. See how many words you can make out of the letters in Santa Claus.

   S-A-N-T-A C-L-A-U-S

4. List four different things you could do to help someone at Christmas time. Draw a picture of what you will do.

5. Draw a big Christmas stocking. Draw toys to put inside of it to surprise someone else. Write the names of the toys on the outside of the stocking.

6. Make up your favorite Christmas recipe. Write down all the ingredients and the directions on how to make it.

7. Using the tune of "Mary Had a Little Lamb," make up a Christmas song. Write it down and sing it to one person.

8. Unscramble these ingredients that can be put in Christmas Cookies.

   fulor   urags   lmki   tubert   stun   gseg

9. Santa has these toys in his bag. What does he have? Finish the words.

   tr____   ba____   sl____   sk____   dr____

   What else could he have that starts with:

   m____   j____   k____   g____   z____

10. Write a letter to Santa. Tell him what you want and why you think you deserve it.

Christmas Tree Math

Materials: 12" X 18" green construction paper, star stickers, colored cereal, glue, crayons or markers

Directions: Each child will draw a large Christmas tree on green construction paper. Write a number or equation at the top of the tree. (Give each child a number appropriate to his/her math level.) They will need to glue the same number of colored cereal and stars on their tree to equal the number or the equation. For instance, if the child's number is 9, he/she will need four pieces of colored cereal and five stars to glue on the tree; or any combination that equals nine. They may continue to decorate the tree with crayon or marker garlands. Trade trees with a partner and count to check the number of objects put on the tree.

Variations:

1. Number the branches on the tree.

2. Give the children a small pile of cereal and let them glue it on the tree for decorations. Then count all the cereal and write the numeral at the top of the tree.

3. Put a different equation on each branch and decorate the branches with the correct number of cereal.

Candy Cane Patterns

Preparation: Cut eight 1" red and eight 1" white construction paper squares per student. Cut one 9" X 6" dark blue or black construction paper per student.

Materials: white and red construction paper squares; dark blue or black paper; glue

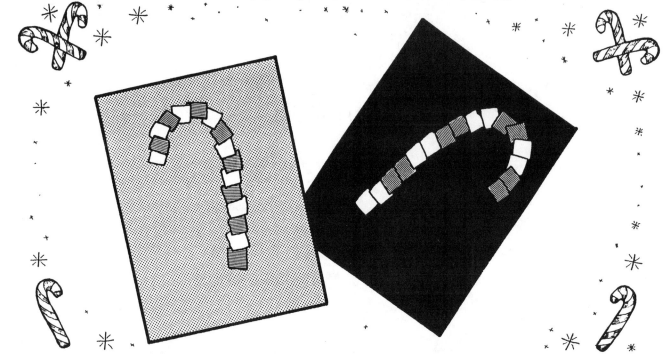

Directions: Give each child eight red and eight white squares and one dark blue or black paper. They will need to make a candy cane with a definite pattern and glue it on their papers. Have them "read" the pattern to you before they glue it down.

Oral Math Problems

Directions: Call out these story problems anytime you have a spare moment. When children are waiting in line, lining up, or waiting for the bus, use those teaching moments to strengthen math skills.

1. Two reindeer, plus two more reindeer make how many altogether?

2. Santa took three elves with him in the sleigh. How many people in all were in the sleigh?

3. I found five Christmas trees, but I lost one. How many were left?

4. Teeka found five of the wild reindeer, but she could not find the other three. How many was she looking for in all?

5. Teeka started back to the North Pole with all eight reindeer, but four ran away. How many were left?

6. If I buy ten Christmas gifts and give away only five, how many will I have left?

7. My uncle is giving me two gifts, my Grandma is giving me two gifts, and my parents are giving me two gifts. How many gifts am I getting all together?

Reindeer Antler Math

Preparation: Make one copy of the reindeer on page 56 for each student. Use some or all of these activities.

1. Count the number of antler branches on the reindeer. Write the numbers on each antler branch.

2. Number the antler branches by 2's.

3. Write an equation on each antler and trade papers with a partner. Write down the answers to your partner's equations. Trade back papers and check your partner's work.

4. Copy equations from the chalkboard. Put one equation on each antler branch. Answer the questions on the antler branch.

5. Work with a partner. One person tells story problems and one person writes the equations and answers on the antlers. Trade.

6. As the teacher tells story problems, write the equation on an antler.

7. Write one number at the base of each antler. Trade papers with a partner. They must make up an equation using the number you wrote as the answer to their equation.

Reindeer Picture

Connect the Dots

Connect the dots to find out what Santa is looking at.

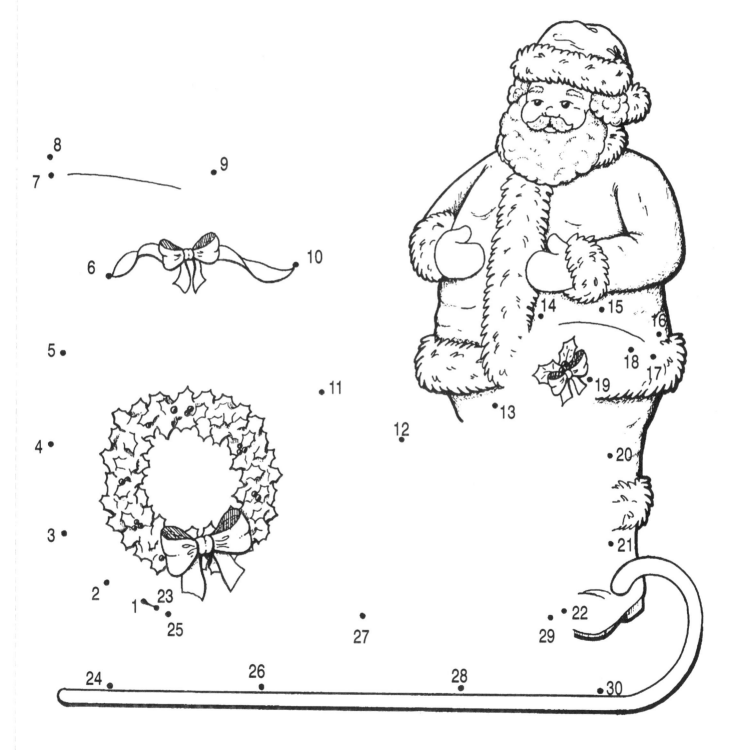

Animal Games
Animal Habitats

In *Night Tree* the family left food on and around the tree for many different animals. Which of those animals do we have in our part of the country?

Preparation: Copy, color, glue on tagboard, cut and laminate the cards on page 60. Make another copy of the cards for each student so they can make their own set of cards to take home. Prepare three 8" X 5" index cards with the following on each card:

Animals We've Seen	Animals to Look For	Animals at the Zoo

Materials: cards on page 60, bulletin board space, push pins

Directions: Discuss which animals might live in your area. Which of these animals belongs in each category? Have the students place the cards in the proper category on the bulletin board.

Wildlife Concentration: Birds or Mammals

Materials: cards from pages 60.

Directions: Discuss the two types of animals seen on the cards and in *Night Tree*. What are the characteristics of birds and mammals? Discuss. Shuffle the cards and place them face down in rows of four by four. Each player flips over two cards, leaving them in the original position. If the cards show the same type of animal (i.e., two mammals—bears and deer), he/she keeps those cards and takes another turn. If the cards don't match, the player puts them face down on the same spot and the next player takes a turn. The object is to capture the most cards by concentrating on where each card is placed.

Animal Games *(cont.)*
Wildlife Bingo

Materials: wildlife Bingo card (below) and animal cards (page 60) for each student; glue; scissors; crayons; markers (i.e., cereal, beans, counters, etc.)

Directions: Color and cut out the animals on page 60. Students glue down the animals in any order on their Bingo card leaving one square as a Free Square. As the teacher calls out an animal name the child locates that animal and places a marker on the animal. The first child to get a line of markers either vertically, horizontally, or diagonally is the winner.

Animal Cards

To be used with pages 58 and 59.

Winter Weather Experiments

What Is the Difference Between Snow and Sleet?

Materials: white frost from the inside of a freezer or snow from the ground; an ice cube; a magnifying glass; black construction paper; a metal spoon or table knife (Have enough frost, ice cubes, and magnifying glasses to give each group of four children one set.)

Directions: Place the frost or snow on a piece of black construction paper and look at it with the magnifying glass. With the spoon or knife, chip off a small piece of the ice cube. Place it on the black construction paper and look at it with the magnifying glass. What do you see? Are they different?

Information: The frost or snow will be a six-pointed crystal. The ice cube will not have this formation. Frost in the refrigerator and snowflakes form the same way. Water vapor in the refrigerator and water vapor in the clouds cool down so fast that they turn into snowflakes and frost. The ice cube starts as water and later freezes. Sleet starts as water or raindrops and when it falls through very cold air it freezes into little bits of ice.

Extension: Have the children perform this experiment at home and show their parents the difference between snow and sleet.

Snowy Day Experiment

You will need to do this experiment after snow has fallen.

Materials: a snowy day; a piece of aluminum foil; a piece of black cloth (The black cloth and the foil need to be the same size, approximately 10" X 10".)

Directions: Put the black cloth and the foil ten inches apart on top of the snow in an area that will get sun. After they have been in the sun one hour, check them to see what has happened.

Information: The black cloth will absorb more heat and sink deeper in the snow. It absorbs more light which turns into heat and melts the snow. The foil reflects the light before it turns into heat.

Extension: Try this experiment with white paper rather than foil. What happens? Let the children decide what other materials they would like to use.

Pop-Up Christmas Place Cards

Materials: 3" X 5" index cards; scissors; crayons or markers; glue; pictures below

Directions: Fold the index card in half widthwise. Trace or glue one of the pictures below onto your card, or make your own Christmas design on each card. Make sure part of the picture is above the fold. Color your picture. Cut around the part of the picture that is above the fold. This part will "pop up." Write the names of your family or guests on the bottom of each card.

Variations:

1. Scramble the guests' names on their cards. They will need to unscramble their names so they can find their places at the table. (i.e., AETK = KATE)

2. Have the children use a math code and write the names in code for their guests to unscramble.
   For example:

Code Chart		Problems on nametags
5 =	Elsa	2+2+1 =
10 =	Imants	20-10 =
8 =	Karl	5 + 3 =
4 =	Erik	9 - 5 =

This type of problem writing gives children lots of practice in writing equations. It can be geared to any level of mathematics you are studying.

Stained Glass Christmas Tree

Materials: tree pattern; oaktag; different colored tissue paper cut in pieces approximately 4" X 3"; glue; green construction paper; scissors

Preparation: Trace the tree pattern below on tagboard. Cut out.

Directions: Trace around the oaktag pattern on green tissue paper. Cut out. Glue the tissue paper on the back of the tree. Hang your tree up in a window and let the light shine through.

Christmas Paper Crackers

These crackers were popular in France in the middle 1800's. They are still popular in England, Canada, and Australia. Two children grab one cracker and tug at opposite ends until the cracker bursts, scattering the contents. Watch the children scramble to pick up the goodies!

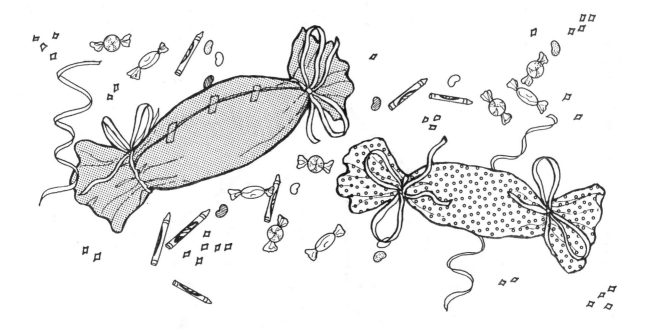

Materials: gift wrap paper or tissue paper; clear tape; ribbon or yarn; scissors; small candies

Directions: Cut wrapping paper into 10" X 6" sheets. Overlap ½ inch on the two 10 inch sides and seal with tape. Slip 12 candies in one end and push them toward the middle. Twist each end of the paper, 3 inches in from the end. Tie the ends at the twisted part with the ribbon. Open each end so that it flares outward, and push inward on the twisted part so the center of the cracker puffs out. Candies will rattle inside the cracker.

Variations: Make these crackers with small toys inside the crackers in place of candy or put crayons, stickers, etc., inside.

Extensions

Writing: Have the children make crackers and then place them in the center of the circle in a big pile or in a large bowl. Let each child pick out another cracker, not his/her own, to open. Before opening, each child must write about what might be in the cracker and illustrate the writing.

Math: After opening the cracker with a friend, they may count the candies or objects in the cracker. Then together they will make up math equations using the objects; i.e., 2 candies plus 3 more candies = 5 candies. After grouping the candies into equations, they can write the equations down either on paper or on the chalkboard.

Language: Tell a story about one of the items in the cracker. Where did it come from? Does it want to be eaten? Where would it like to be? Does it have a candy friend? Tell your story to your partner.

Reindeer Antler Hat

Directions: Cut out using brown construction paper. Attach to 2" x 24" piece of brown construction paper to make a reindeer antler hat. Adjust to fit child's head.

Art

Triangle Reindeer

Materials: cotton swabs; brown crayon; 9" x 11" brown construction paper; white scraps of paper; 9" x 11" black construction paper; glue; scissors; red tissue paper

Directions: Demonstrate drawing a large triangle on the brown paper for the face. Draw two smaller triangles for the ears. Draw two circles on the white paper for the eyes and two smaller brown circles for the center of the eyes. Wad up the tissue paper to make a nose. Glue the large brown triangle on black paper, add triangle ears, circle eyes, and tissue paper nose. Color the sticks of the cotton swabs brown and glue on the top of the head for antlers.

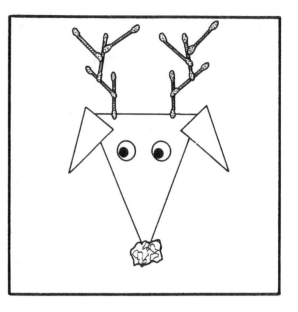

Writing Extension: Make up a name for your reindeer. Tell a story about it. Where is it going? What does it eat? Is it tame or wild? Can you ride on it? Will it come to you when you call it? How many triangles did you use to make it?

Paper-Tube Kazoo

Materials: one toilet paper roll per person; tissue paper or wax paper; rubber bands; pencil or scissors

Directions: Cut out a piece of wax paper or tissue paper approximately 4" X 4". Place it over one end of the paper tube and hold it in place with a rubber band. Punch a hole in the side of the tube near the covered end. Use a pencil or scissors to punch the hole. Be gentle. The tube will collapse if you punch with too much force.

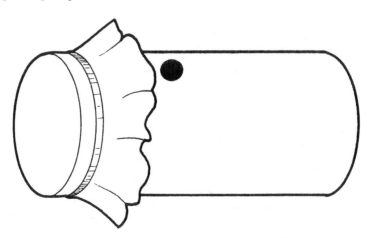

How to Use: Place the open end of the tube near your mouth and hum or sing into the tube. The paper at the other end vibrates and you have a kazoo. Try singing "Rudolph the Red-Nosed Reindeer" and "We Wish You a Merry Christmas."

Triangle Santa

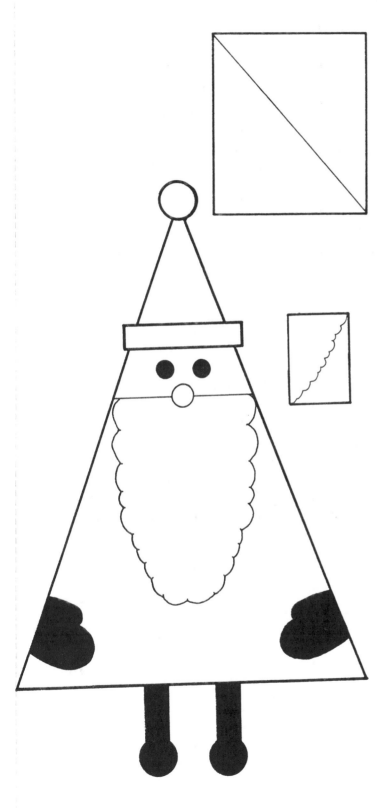

Materials: red butcher paper cut into 20" squares (one per child); 9" X 12" white and black construction paper (one of each color per child); small pink piece of construction paper; scissors; glue; pencil; chalk

Directions: Give each child one red piece of butcher paper, one black and one white piece of construction paper, and a scrap of pink paper.

1. Fold the red butcher paper in half. Show the children how to draw a diagonal line from the inside edge to the lower corner. Cut on this line to make a red triangle. This will be Santa's body.

2. Cut one $1/2$ inch strip from the short side of the white construction paper for the hat brim. Fold the white paper in half length wise and show the children how to draw a scallop shape for a beard. Cut out. Using the leftover white scraps cut one big circle for the top of Santa's hat.

3. Place hands on the top part of the black construction paper and trace around them with fingers together to make Santa's mittens.

4. On the black paper draw two rectangles with circles on the ends for Santa's feet.

5. Draw two more black circles for Santa's eyes.

6. Draw another circle on the pink paper for Santa's nose.

7. Glue everything in place.

Extension: Use this same idea and reduce the size. Put your triangle Santa on the front of a Christmas card.

Christmas Placemats

Materials: red and green 12" X 18" construction paper; rulers; scissors; paper scraps and/or fabric scraps; glue; pictures of patchwork quilts or mats that have a pattern; lamination or contact paper

Directions: Ask the children to divide two 12" X 18" papers into squares. Each square should be the same size. Have the children figure out how to do this with their rulers and pencils. This will require some math and they may need help figuring this out. (Younger children might need to fold the paper in half and then keep folding until they get squares.)

On one of the 12" X 18" papers, draw a pattern in the squares. Keep it simple and repeat the pattern. For example, star, triangle, square, star, triangle, square, or any other simple design. When you have decided on your pattern, cut out the shapes and use those for patterns or glue these shapes on the other sheet. If you are using the shapes for patterns, trace around the patterns on paper or fabric.

The other sheet of red or green paper that has been divided into squares will be used as the background for your placemat. Lay your pieces on the squares. Be sure it forms a pattern. Glue them down. If lamination is available, laminate the placemats before the children take them home. If lamination is not available, cover them with clear contact paper.

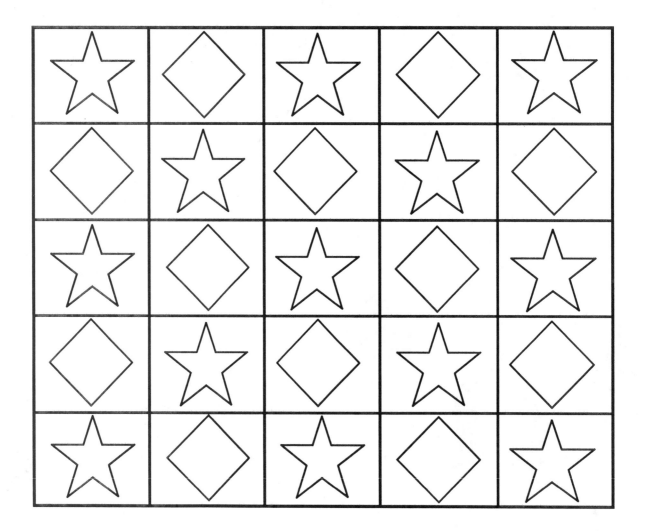

Pop-up Christmas Card

Color, cut, and fold the hat down inside the card. When the card opens, the hat will pop up. Write a message inside.

Sing a Song

"You Are My Reindeer"

Tune: *"You Are My Sunshine"*

You are my reindeer,
My wild reindeer.
You make me angry
When you won't mind.

You are my reindeer,
My wild reindeer.
Please don't run
away again!

You are my reindeer,
My wild reindeer.
What will I do
with all of you?

Santa will need you
On Christmas Eve.
I can't train you,
My wild reindeer.

You are my reindeer,
My wild reindeer.
I'm learning to be
so kind to you.

We are becoming
very good friends.
Santa will be so
Proud of you.

"Let's All Decorate the Night Tree"

Tune: *"We Wish You a Merry Christmas"*

Let's all decorate the Night Tree.
Let's all decorate the Night Tree.
Let's all decorate the Night Tree.
And give our animal friends a treat.

Let's hang up some popcorn chains.
Let's hang up some popcorn chains.
Let's hang up some popcorn chains.
And give our animal friends a treat.

3. Let's hang up apples and tangerines.

4. Let's scatter nuts and breadcrumbs.

Sing a Song *(cont.)*

"The Wheels on the Train"

Tune: *"The Wheels on the Bus"*

The wheels on the train
Go 'round and 'round,
'Round and 'round,
'Round and 'round.

The wheels on the train
Go 'round and 'round,
All the way to
The North Pole.

2. The conductor on the train
   Says "All Aboard,"

3. The whistle on the train
   Goes toot, toot, toot

4. The steam on the train
   Goes hiss, hiss, hiss

5. The children on the train
   Laugh and eat

6. The children on the train
   See Santa Claus .....
   At the North Pole.

Add rhythm instruments for sound effects. Sand blocks for the hiss sound, whistles, bells, and tambourines for the train whistle, and sticks for the sound of the trains wheels clicking along the track.

Add hand motions for the wheels going 'round and 'round by making hands go in a circle around each other. Cup hands around mouth to shout "All Aboard." Act out laughing and eating.

Reindeer Movement

Using reindeer hats children made (page 65), have them pretend they are reindeer. Discuss how reindeer move. Let the children demonstrate walking, running, leaping, galloping, jumping, and prancing. Play fast music and let children move like reindeer. Call out the different movements and let them demonstrate each.

Cooking

Banana Malted Milkshakes

When the boy boarded the Polar Express they fed him candy and hot chocolate. We will serve Banana Malted Milkshakes on our train.

Ingredients:
1 gallon milk
1 gallon vanilla ice cream
$^3/_4$ cup malt
3 ripe bananas

Equipment: Blender
Spoon
Paper cups (one per child)

Directions: Spoon some ice cream into the blender. Pour in some milk and 1 T. of the malt. Add $^1/_2$ banana and blend together. If the mixture appears too thick, add more milk. If it appears to be too thin, add more ice cream. Pour into cups and serve. Repeat until all children have had a serving.

Variations:

- Add 1 teaspoon chocolate syrup to the mixture to make a chocolate drink.
- Add 1 teaspoon strawberry jam to make a strawberry drink.
- Let the children make up other variations of the drink.
- Make the drink and leave out the malt.

Fox Sandwiches

Make this after reading *Night Tree*. In *Night Tree*, one of the animals that the boy imagines will come to the tree is a fox.

Ingredients:
hot dogs (one per student)
bread (two slices per student)
cheese (one slice per student)
margarine
catsup (in a squeeze bottle)

Equipment: small container to melt
    margarine
pastry brush or paper towel
cookie sheet
knife
toothpicks
round 2 $^1/_2$ inch cookie cutter or
    cardboard template to trace
    around

Directions: Cut the hot dog in half lengthwise. Make a cheese sandwich with 2 slices of bread and a piece of cheese in between. Using the cookie cutter or the template, cut the sandwich into a circle. Wrap the hot dog halves around the sandwich and fasten together with toothpicks. Grease a cookie sheet with margarine and place the sandwiches on the sheet. Brush them with melted margarine. Make a catsup fox face. Bake the sandwiches at 400 degrees for 5 minutes. Bake the leftovers, too.

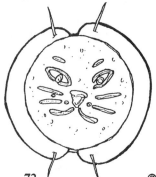

     72

Cooking (cont.)

Luscious Christmas Lollipops

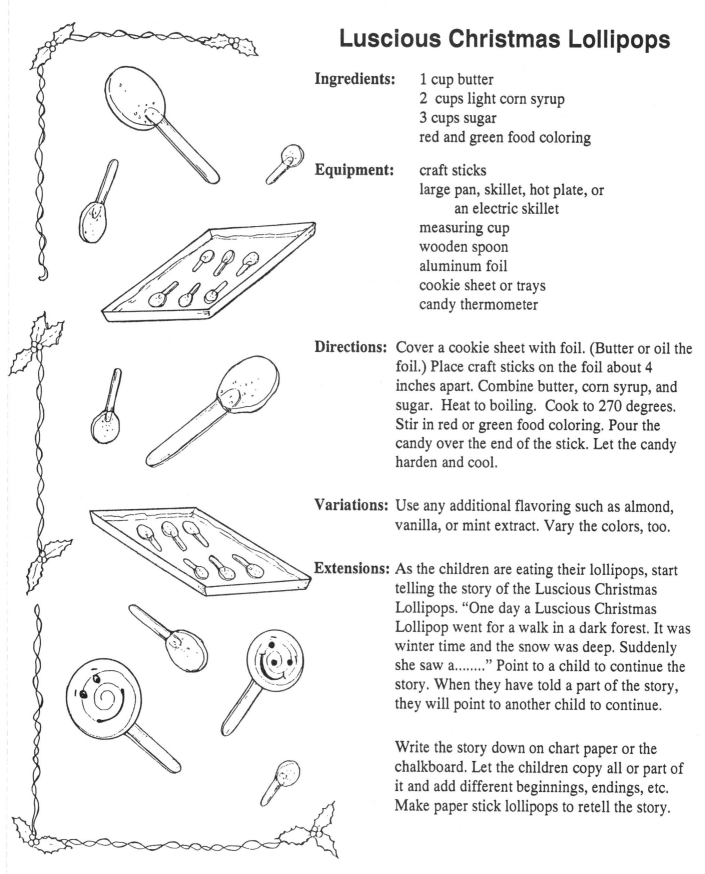

Ingredients: 1 cup butter
2 cups light corn syrup
3 cups sugar
red and green food coloring

Equipment: craft sticks
large pan, skillet, hot plate, or
    an electric skillet
measuring cup
wooden spoon
aluminum foil
cookie sheet or trays
candy thermometer

Directions: Cover a cookie sheet with foil. (Butter or oil the foil.) Place craft sticks on the foil about 4 inches apart. Combine butter, corn syrup, and sugar. Heat to boiling. Cook to 270 degrees. Stir in red or green food coloring. Pour the candy over the end of the stick. Let the candy harden and cool.

Variations: Use any additional flavoring such as almond, vanilla, or mint extract. Vary the colors, too.

Extensions: As the children are eating their lollipops, start telling the story of the Luscious Christmas Lollipops. "One day a Luscious Christmas Lollipop went for a walk in a dark forest. It was winter time and the snow was deep. Suddenly she saw a........" Point to a child to continue the story. When they have told a part of the story, they will point to another child to continue.

Write the story down on chart paper or the chalkboard. Let the children copy all or part of it and add different beginnings, endings, etc. Make paper stick lollipops to retell the story.

Cooking *(cont.)*

Christmas Popsicles

Ingredients:
1 quart yogurt
l large can frozen cranberry juice
1 T. vanilla
¼ cup honey

Equipment: small paper cups or popsicle molds
(one per student)
craft sticks (one per student)
large spoon and bowl

Directions: Let the children take turns mixing the yogurt and juice together. When thoroughly mixed, add vanilla and honey. Mix again. Fill paper cups half full and place a popsicle stick in the center of each cup. Freeze until hard. To eat, tear the cup away from the popsicle and ENJOY!

Variation: Make green popsicles by using lime juice in place of cranberry juice and adding more honey.

Extensions:

- Print the recipe on the chalkboard or chart paper and let them copy it to take home. Have them illustrate their recipe with pictures of the cooking process or the finished product.

- Let the children write in their journals the different steps used to make the popsicles.

- Write the directions on how to mix the recipe on tagboard. Cut up the sentences and let the children place the sentences in the correct order in a pocket chart.

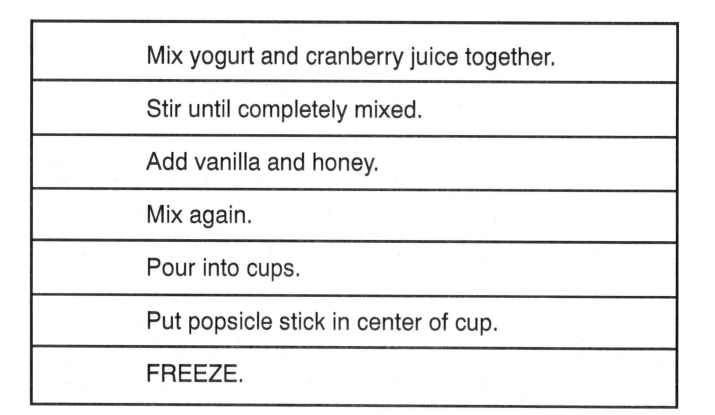

Mix yogurt and cranberry juice together.
Stir until completely mixed.
Add vanilla and honey.
Mix again.
Pour into cups.
Put popsicle stick in center of cup.
FREEZE.

Class Pillow

Make a large pillow celebrating the books in this thematic unit. Let children use it in the classroom library center as they enjoy reading.

Materials: approximately 2 ½ yards of white, beige or light colored fabric, permanent marking pens or fabric crayons (fabric crayons can be purchased at dime stores, fabric stores, or craft stores.); 8" X 8" squares of typing paper; batting or filling for the pillow; iron

Directions: Each child will need to pick a Christmas book he/she would like to illustrate. For example: draw a train from *The Polar Express*, a tree from *Night Tree*, or a reindeer from *The Wild Christmas Reindeer.* On the typing paper, draw a sketch with a pencil. If you are using markers, trace this sketch on a corner of the fabric and color with markers. If you are using fabric crayons, sketch the picture on the typing paper and color it with the fabric crayons. This will be transferred to the fabric by ironing it on. (See directions on the fabric crayons.)

When all the children's pictures are on the fabric, sew and stuff the pillow. (A parent volunteer would be helpful for this.) Place it in the library or listening center for the children to use and enjoy.

Variations: Using the same idea, the children can make class or individual wall hangings. In addition to the above supplies, you would need a dowel rod, tube, or wire hangers to hang up the wall hanging. Class quilts can be made using the same idea. The children love to see their work displayed in a permanent place in the school or your classroom.

Going to the North Pole Game
(2-4 players)

To play this game, you will need markers and 1 die. Place the markers on Start. Roll dice. Move ahead that number of spaces. If you land on a town, village, tunnel, bridge, or forest, you don't need to do anything. Try to do everything you're asked to do on the other spaces. If you can't do something, ask another player to help you. The first person to get to the North Pole gets the first gift from Santa Claus.

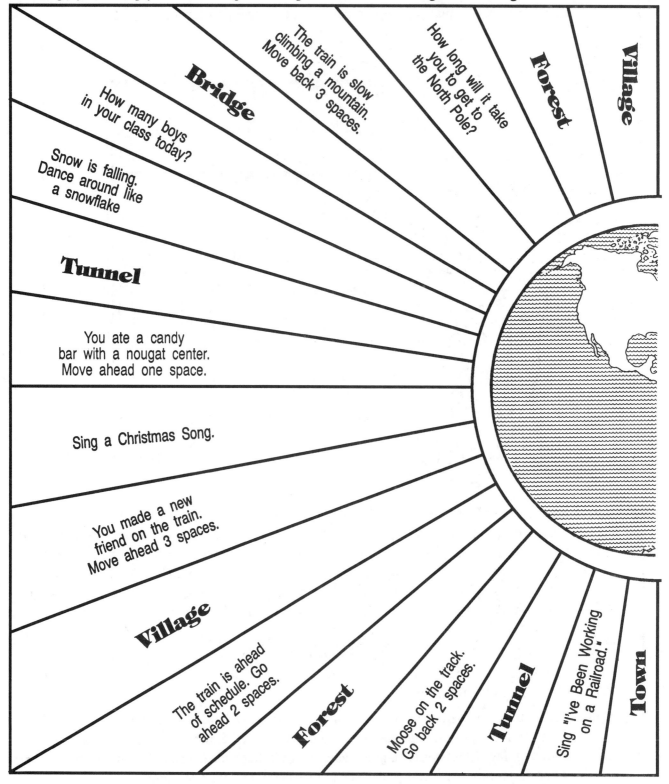

Village

Forest

How long will it take you to get to the North Pole?

The train is slow climbing a mountain. Move back 3 spaces.

Bridge

How many boys in your class today?

Snow is falling. Dance around like a snowflake

Tunnel

You ate a candy bar with a nougat center. Move ahead one space.

Sing a Christmas Song.

You made a new friend on the train. Move ahead 3 spaces.

Village

The train is ahead of schedule. Go ahead 2 spaces.

Forest

Moose on the track. Go back 2 spaces.

Tunnel

Sing "I've Been Working on a Railroad."

Town

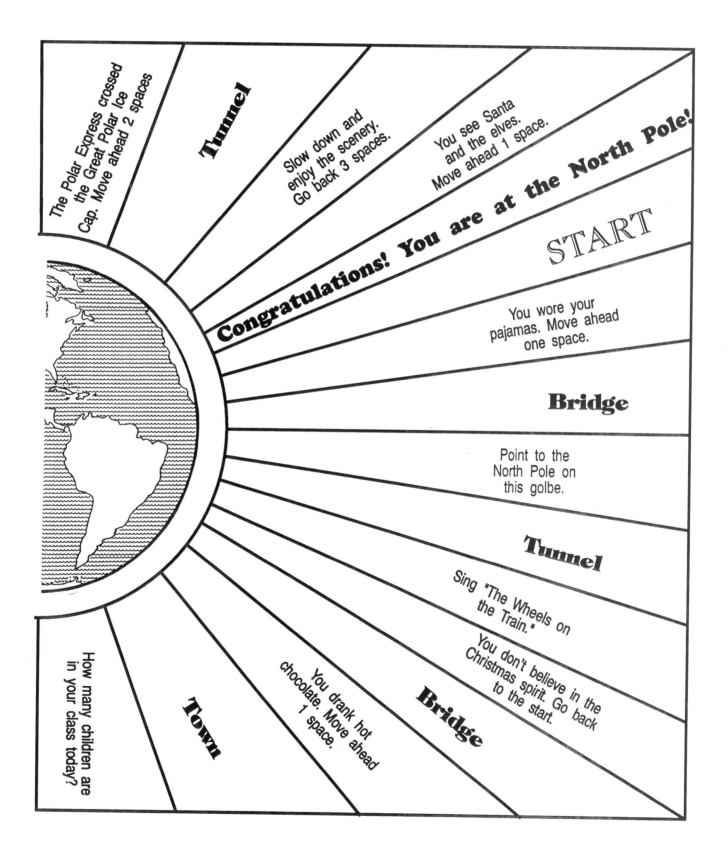

The Polar Express crossed the Great Polar Ice Cap. Move ahead 2 spaces

Tunnel

Slow down and enjoy the scenery. Go back 3 spaces.

You see Santa and the elves. Move ahead 1 space.

Congratulations! You are at the North Pole!

START

You wore your pajamas. Move ahead one space.

Bridge

Point to the North Pole on this golbe.

Tunnel

Sing "The Wheels on the Train."

You don't believe in the Christmas spirit. Go back to the start.

Bridge

You drank hot chocolate. Move ahead 1 space.

Town

How many children are in your class today?

Dear Parents,

If you are in need of ideas for stocking stuffers or gifts that will help your child academically or strengthen small and large motor skills, look over the following list:

- ABC rubber stamps and stamp pad
- individual chalkboards, chalk, and eraser
- 10-50 piece puzzles
- jump ropes, balls, frisbees, bean bags
- bingo games
- number or ABC flash cards
- dominoes
- small bulletin board
- clay, rolling pin, ABC or number cookie cutters
- scrapbook or notebook to keep special papers
- rhyming games, number games
- marking pens, new crayons, scissors, glue
- a play clock
- deck of cards or any card game
- puppets
- lace-up-cards
- And of course BOOKS, BOOKS BOOKS!

Sincerely,

_____

78

December Clip Art

Bibliography

Core Books

Bunting, Eve. *Night Tree.* (Harcourt Brace Jovanovich, 1991)

Brett, Jan. *The Wild Christmas Reindeer.* (G. P. Putnam's Sons, 1990)

Van Allsburg, Chris. *The Polar Express.* (Houghton Mifflin, 1985)

Fiction Books

Adams, Adrienne. *The Christmas Party.* (Charles Scribner's, 1978)

Ahlberg, Janet & Allan. *The Jolly Christmas Postman.* (Little, 1991)

Aliki. *Christmas Tree Memories.* (Harper Collins, 1991)

Brown, Michael. *Santa Mouse.* (Crosset & Dunlap, 1966)

Hazen, Barbara. *Rudolph The Red-Nosed Reindeer.* (Golden Press, 1964)

Herriot, James. *The Christmas Day Kitten.* (St. Martin's Press, 1976)

Keats, Ezra Jack. *The Little Drummer Boy.* (Scholastic, 1968)

Kunnas, Mauri. *Santa Claus and His Elves.* (Harmony, 1981)

Moore, Clement C. *The Night Before Christmas.* (Scholastic, 1985)

Ray, Jane. *The Story of Christmas.* (Dutton, 1991)

Say, Allen. *Tree of Cranes.* (Houghton, 1991)

Stevenson, James. *The Worst Person's Christmas.* (Greenwillow, 1991)

Wells, Rosemary. *Morris's Disappearing Bag.* (Children's Choice, 1975)

Yolen, Jane & dePaola, Tomie. *Hark! A Christmas Sampler.* (G.P. Putnams, 1991)

Non-Fiction

Baker, Susan. *The Christmas Book.* (Grosset & Dunlap, 1979)

Behrens, June. *Hanukkah.* (Childrens Press, 1983)

Carey, Diana & Large, Judy. *Festivals, Family & Food.* (Hawthorn, 1982)

Chaikin, Miriam. *Hanukkah.* (Holiday House, 1990)

dePaola, Tomie. *The Family Christmas Tree Book.* (Holiday House, 1980)

Fowler, Virginie. *Christmas Crafts & Customs.* (Prentice-Hall, 1984)

Kelley, Emily. *Christmas Around the World.* (Carolrhoda, 1986)

Patent, Dorothy Hinshaw. *Christmas Trees.* (Dodd, Mead & Company, 1987)

Stevens, Patricia Bunning. *Merry Christmas, A History of the Holiday.* (Macmillan, 1979)

Wright-Baltzell, Linda. *Christmas is Coming.* (Oxmoor House, 1991)